Dear Dad

Dear Dad Book Excerpts Highlights

"You know? Family politics can be a straight bitch. It can flow deep. And it can cut deep. You have to understand what I'm calling *family politics*. It was family politics that gave me all of the growing-up experiences I have detailed in this book."

"This cold war that gets waged on the inside of our family between the so-called legitimate and the somehow perceived illegitimate sibling is madness. It's ignorance, and it is so not our father. *That* is someone else. And that shit motivates me because sometimes how I see it as, *Oh, I'm not supposed to win. Okay. I'm going to push even more.* And push to the top. "Never ever back down" is how I was raised. Challenge is no stranger to me. And there is no fear of challenge. But there is so much challenge out here in life that the last place you want to see it come from is inside of your family, whether it is a cold war or a hot one."

"Sometimes it feels as though that support I have from my Marley family is conditional or that there is support only when I'm doing exactly what is expected of me by some members of my family."

"And when I say, "support," when it comes to a family like mine, it means a lot on myriad levels—because of the power my family members wield. It's not just like your brother coming to you, giving you a slap on the back, and saying, "Hey, I support you." My family is well established in my industry; my family members have ways in which they can lend support and cause an effect, and they have ways that they can make themselves felt in a vacuum of support. The impact of sentiment and attitudes happen on a huger level, for sure. But even just that slap on the back is worth something at times. I'd be happy for that if it were sincere and from love."

"It was not like any true paternal question lingered as to how I came about or whom I belonged to. Even when I was back in Jamaica, right after my pops had passed away, the family used to travel through the country and they would sometimes stop and see me—not too often, but maybe twice in a year. They'd come to my little town, or I'd go to Kingston and stay for a week or two and then I'd come back home to where we lived. So my paternity must have been acknowledged. These were clearly my brothers and sisters. We would play together and eat together. We knew one another the whole time we were growing up. It wasn't like I was this kid who just showed up on the doorstep one day. So that couldn't be a justification for my mom and I being financially cut off, as if I died when my father died."

"But when I would visit my siblings, it was like night and day. My brothers were staying' where my dad stayed, naturally. So that house was a very big house. That house was three stories, had a pool . . . you name it. They lived on the top of the hill. Everything you could want in the house, it was there. Rehearsal room, gym, different bedrooms, a farm, all kinds of shit; and I'd be coming back home from two weeks of helpers, cooks, gardeners, and a lawn man to bathing and cooking outside in our front yard in Falmouth."

"I was growing up, and I was wising up. Even if my mom and I were only getting a damn $300 to $400 a month, that shit would have been great for us and would have made all of the difference. At least we would have had that to look forward to. It was a multi-multi-multi-million-dollar estate. And nobody could ask if I needed a book bag?"

"The day had come, and we were ready to move forward. Finally, I was told by the estate, "Okay, you can have this lump sum of money. But if you take the lump sum of money, you're going to have to invest it all back into the estate in full. And we will give you (something like) three g's a month and a 60k payout for your bank account to start." Looking back, that's some old monkey money if you ask me. Then I was told, "If you choose *not* to invest the full amount back into the estate, you can no longer be a part of the estate," meaning its earnings. Okay. Wow. So here I am. I didn't know the ins and outs of the estate business."

"Then, I looked at my brothers and my sisters, who were talking about this money and putting it back. I'm saying, *For real. What would you do?* I heard all of these voices and concerns in my head, and I thought, *Whoa. So if I don't give this money right back to you, that you just gave to me after all these years, now I'm no longer a part of the estate like I'm no longer a son of my own dad?* How could I no longer be a part of an estate whose earnings were based on my father's work, legacy, and intellectual properties? All of them could keep living on my father's earnings, but I couldn't? How does that work? And they wanted it *all* back—not half, not a quarter, all. "

"Plus the voices were running down to me on the other side that this pay-it-back option wasn't coming with any paperwork— meaning I just had people talking to me about something that I was supposed to just take at face value. There was no security in a decision like that for me. So I decided I was not going to do that. I was just going to take my share out of it. I kept the money. I didn't reinvest or give all the money back that they had just handed to me—which was what they wanted to me to do. But, that's okay."

"I had brothers and sisters who were upset with me, and they stopped talking to me. Period. I couldn't believe this. My perspective about it was, *here you are telling me to return this money. But there you have been for your entire frickin' life spending money like there's no tomorrow. And the money you're spending, it's not like that's all money that you went out and earned on your own; a lot of it is still "our" father's money. So now, you can't be upset with me because for the first time I'm gonna be able to experience life a little differently—and this is something that you have been doing all along.*"

Dear Dad

By Ky-Mani Marley

Farrah Gray Publishing

www.fgpbooks.com

Farrah Gray Publishing, its logos, and its marks are trademarks of Farrah Gray Publishing

Publisher: Farrah Gray Publishing
P.O. Box 33355
Las Vegas, NV 89133

Cover Photos Mike Prior and Roberto Chamorro
Cover Deisgn Kimiyo Nishio
Author Ky-Mani Marley with Andre Akil and Danielle Jean-Jacques
Interior design and formatting by Lawna Patterson Oldfield

Contents

**An Open Letter from Publisher
Dr. Farrah Gray**   page xi

Prologue   page xv

CHAPTER 1
First World   page 1

CHAPTER 2
Ya Fadda Dead   page 27

CHAPTER 3
Mother's Milk   page 43

CHAPTER 4
Broken Promised Land   page 57

CHAPTER 5

Very Rude Boy page 69
(Unnecessary Badness)

CHAPTER 6

Crack Got No Clock page 95
(Unnecessary Badness 2)

CHAPTER 7

Never Back Down page 111
(Unnecessary Badness 3)

CHAPTER 8

*"You neglected, Rejected and
Ejected Me . . . Still Its
Only Love I Have"* page 135

CHAPTER 9

Many Mansions in My Father's House page 175

CHAPTER 10

Life From Both Sides page 195
(www.LoveOverAll.org)

Ky-Mani Marley Songs-Lyrics page 213

An Open Letter from Publisher Dr. Farrah Gray

WHAT AN EXTRAORDINARY EXPERIENCE IT HAS BEEN. Farrah Gray Publishing, Inc. is finally established and ready to make history. When I took on this challenge of launching our own publishing company, it took me back to the many companies/businesses I'd launched before and nurtured from concept to fruition. But I had no idea that this one would turn into the all-consuming venture that it has. I have a new respect for those publishing titans who first worked to make my own publications a success around the world, actually bringing my message to the globe in nine different languages. Amazing. And now . . . I must pay it forward.

Today I stand poised to do for others exactly what was done for me, by helping to get worthy motivational, educational, and inspirational voices out into the world. I want to give voices of contribution a higher platform to sound their messages and perspectives to the world in a way that helps to increase the common good and common value of us all.

Enter Ky-Mani Marley. When I first met Ky-Mani Marley, I was humbled and completely aware I was meeting cultural royalty. Bob Marley is, inarguably, the greatest icon of reggae music around the world, with an inspirational legacy for social justice, unity, and "one love" for all. In fact, according to *Fortune Magazine*, the Marley legacy is so revered around the world that the Marley Estate is expected to generate worldwide annual sales in excess of $1 billion by 2012. The late Bob Marley's brand and music have surpassed those of Michael Jackson, Elvis, John Lennon, and Jimmy Hendrix. His message is known by countless millions of people in nations across the globe. Any son of Marley is the son of a king, and automatically a prince in his own right. I was most aware that the moment was special.

I had already known Ky-Mani's music, being a reggae-music fan all of my life. However, as I began to discover Ky-Mani's unique story and upbringing, I stopped in my tracks. He didn't grow up the way you might think a Marley would. He told me that his personal fight to excel from abject poverty to a Grammy Award-nominated reggae artist himself wasn't an inheritance . . . it was a story of struggle, survival, and, finally, success.

As Ky-Mani went on to share more about his music, his message, his philanthropic work, and his overall mission to the world, it was clear that he was directly shaped by his early struggles and redemptive hardships in life. As this man shared his heartfelt story with me, I knew I had found my first book to publish. I was completely moved. The world had to hear the story that I was hearing. Shortly after our meeting, I presented Mr. Marley with an opportunity to publish his memoir. I wanted to do this for the millions of others who find themselves in impossible situations, but in need of the anchoring strength of resolve to persevere in the face of anything and everything.

Ky-Mani Marley's story and this first book from our new imprint are, I believe, special. The story of determination to succeed is the story of life itself for so many, if not for us all. This cyclical narrative of human history feeds the collective soul of all humanity, no matter the generation or the culture in which we may find ourselves. It is all of our stories in one way or another. I was personally touched by this mother-and-son journey of survival, which ultimately culminated into his philanthropic work and mission to the world today. It is amazing to me how someone who, through much of his life, was seemingly robbed of so much, is far from bitter, and just lives and breathes to give so much back to the world. To me, that is the essence of his dad's heart still alive in him. Sometimes a spiritual inheritance is much more priceless than a financial one.

We present to you Ky-Mani Marley's *Dear Dad*, the first of many publications we have in store for you.

I am,
Dr. Farrah Gray

Prologue

Mic Check

YOU NEVER KNOW WHOSE SKIN YOU'LL BE BORN INTO. I'm half-famous for my first name. I'm half-famous for my last. I've lived a life that not many know about and that some don't want me to tell about. I am son of an icon. I am son of a king. I am one son of a brood of Marley siblings, true—but I am one with a story that is uniquely my own.

Growing up *"Marley"* has been a blessing to all my brothers and sisters, and to myself. However, for me, growing up Marley may not have been what you imagined or thought it should have been. My rise to the *now* of my life was a unique rise along a unique journey. My royal lineage and inherited legacy has definitely been a sword with a sharpened and dual edge. I was the son of a king. Undisputedly. But I was clearly a son in exile.

As a result, my life turned into a spiral of struggle, rebellion, and at times, raw aggression—the byproduct of years of unaddressed pain. I speculate about and sort the pieces of my own self even now as I recall and remember all that came before this moment.

I woke up during my teenage years and discovered myself floundering, hustling, and selling weed and crack to survive—or maybe just to rebel. By that time it was all the same to me. I was getting older and starting to sense that things weren't right. I was also starting to sense that some things had never been right.

And that's when it hit me.

This is not the life I would have had to live if he were here— my dad. I had spent half my life gurgling, right above drowning, forced to survive outside the gates of my father's kingdom.

If you think I'm here to cry because I wasn't raised in a castle with silk pillows 'n shit, you've got me wrong. Living inside the estate luxuries and enjoying the treasures of my father's kingdom wasn't in the cards for me. I know that now. There was a different plan for Ky-Mani. I am clear that I was born to feel the pulse and the pain of these forgotten people that my father sang about—by growing up as one of them myself. I now know that feeling this struggle up close and personal—feeling this touch intimately—has made me exactly who I am today.

I've done many things that I am not proud of. I've done

many things for which I am proud. I have turned what was largely a destructive lifestyle into a constructive one. I have done this not only for myself but hopefully for the benefit of many.

But, wow.

My life.

It's been a story kept close to the chest for as long as my years here. Not many knew about it. Not many know about it. It may even be news to some of my siblings. But although some of my story is drenched with battle, pain, and difficulty, it is most of all rich with the ultimate redemption of self.

My theory is that *this life serves as a classroom if we let it.* I'm here to tell a story—my human story—for any insight and lesson it provides. My story is only 1 in 6 billion. But maybe there's something in the telling of this story, my own story, that will have an impact on you, that will touch the story of *you.* It's this reason I share my music, my melody, my lyrics, my life. As far as I'm concerned, with the example left by my father, it's just the *Marley* way.

So today, I share with you my personal story with great hopes. I share it with the hope that you may be moved to something more positive by the end of this book than what you possess here at the beginning.

One Love,
Ky-Mani Marley

First World

MY FIRST BREATH OF AMERICAN AIR WAS FILLED WITH THE SCENT OF CRACK COCAINE BURNING ACROSS THE STREET FROM OUR NEW HOME. I was seven years old and newly dropped into a nightmare that was quickly replacing my dream of what America was about—my dream of what coming to America was supposed to be about. I had just awakened from an overnight flight from my Jamaican birthplace and found myself in the supposed "promised land." *Where were the pots of gold that my grandmother had described? How could this be the land where all of our dreams would come true?* If this was the American dream, I wanted to wake the hell up, and wake up now!

From the basers across the street to the rotted-out abandoned cars, from the busted windows to the spray painted graffiti littering my view, I knew I was far away from the island sanctuary that was my first world. The substandard conditions that we were fleeing were starting to look like an all-out paradise to me now, and all I wanted to do was run back. Anything to get away from this madness.

I was ripped from an extremely impoverished but peaceful plot of Jamaican countryside and replanted right in the middle of *Drama Central, U.S.A.*—a concrete jungle in Miami, Florida, with predators and killers lurking at every turn. My first world was vanishing. Going back wasn't going to be an option, I could tell. My whole family had moved to the States. I had a brand-new reality to face—one I wasn't ready for . . . but since when is life concerned about your punk-ass *readiness*?

My first six years of life were quickly fading into the drama of the present and would soon become a memory I could only piece together in my mind. Sometimes, as I got older, just to get away from the realities of my now, I would pinch a grip of Jamaica's finest, sit back, and *remember*.

It was to Falmouth, Trelawny, Jamaica, that I was born on February 26, 1976. After six long solid days of labor, I was finally here and set to do this—blessings to my beloved mother! Now notice all those sixes. If those weren't enough, I was also nameless for six whole weeks until that beautiful woman, Anita Belnavis, finally settled on a proper name for her firstborn baby boy: Ky-Mani (meaning "adventurous traveler"). I'm sure the reason I was left as Baby X for so long was because of her complete and utter exhaustion after labor.

My Moms admits to me now that she was worried about all those damned sixes surrounding my birth: 6 days of labor, on the 26th day of the 76th year, taking 6 weeks to name . . . it made her a little nervous, understandably. But luckily, altogether there were four of them, instead of just three. She clowns me about that to this day, and we still get a good laugh out of it. I can't blame her, though, 'cause on the real, by the time I was sixteen, she was probably worrying about it all over again. By that time I was a whole different creation, doin' my share of dirt on the streets of Miami. Given what my grimy badass was into, I wouldn't have blamed anyone for counting up those sixes *juuuust* to make sure.

I always wondered how it was for my mother to have to see me grow from the sweet little boy she watched playing in the Jamaican sun, to the man who became as cold, wild, and dangerous as the hood environment I would ultimately be raised in. I don't know how much this hurt her, but my choices were few. The choices in that world were to be *predator* or *prey*—*eat* or be *eaten*. And since I'm here still standin' to tell my story, I guess you understand who was doing the frickin' eatin'.

I had some dark days after my Jamaican sun had set—and I don't guess those sixes had anything to do with it. *It was what it was,* and *it is what it is.* I can't control how I showed up in this life. How I got here is how I got here. Now . . . I just *am.* First world to the last world, guess you could say I'm merely here for the journey of it all. Aren't you?

My journey began in Falmouth, Jamaica. While South Africa had its shanty towns and America had its ghettos, 1981 Falmouth also had its little shit-hole for the people they were trying to flush down the toilet. We called it *Compound.* Compound was Falmouth's tenement yard or low budget government housing. You could say it was the shanty town of my first city. Still, it was the first place I called home, and this little town is the place that holds my fondest memories of life. It is the place that makes me who I am today, at the deepest level.

I've got to stop and tell you a little bit of background about this town that was my first home, my first soil, the soil that produced me. Falmouth is a town in Trelawny on the northern coast of Jamaica with a kind of diabolical history when it comes to my African peoples. This is because Falmouth, Trelawny, was absolutely a Boss Town in slavery time. When I read up about it, they call it a *boomtown.* It was the big shit. It was a central hub to the cross-Atlantic slave trade. Millions of us had to fall through and touch Falmouth, no matter where our final destinations were throughout the diaspora—that is if we survived the middle passage, being dragged across that water packed together like fish in a can. That's something really insane when you envision humans being stacked and shipped like a fuckin' DHL or UPS delivery. Makes you think that the people who were doing this needed more help than the people it was being done to.

This first soil of mine was way deep in the hustle of smuggling and selling black African bodies to the New World, which as we know, was already an Old World, of course. It was just new to Chris Columbus and his peeps back in Europe. But anyway, that boy there is another story for another time—he's already had his fifteen minutes of fame in the lies we were taught in his-story class. Did he not?

Like I was saying, Falmouth was a main distribution drop-off for African slaves at that time, and it even ended up being a Boss player in the sugar trade. Huge. Falmouth actually provided sugar to the entire planet and was the world's largest producer of the top commodity at the time. All of this sugar bounty and wealth was harvested at the toil and sweat of African hands in the oppressive island sun. Falmouth was made rich and notable, becoming one of the busiest seaports in Jamaica. The town was balling outta control, right up in the middle of a lot of drama that was detrimental to African peoples.

But Falmouth is my home. And as you can see, Falmouth has been filled with hustlers since the day Sir William Trelawny and the other English settlers set it up—since back when the main product was us. Maybe that's why I've got so much hustle in my blood. My people lived and bled for the hustle until the day the British emancipated their kidnapped labor force. The hustle was literally in the soil and the blood in that soil. And it's on this soil that my story began.

By the time I finally popped outta my momma's belly, after those six days of pain and strain to get me here, I know she was glad to have me out, but boy if she only knew—we were just gettin' started. It was 1976. By then, Falmouth was a town that had more of a history than it looked to have a future. It wasn't *Boss Town* no more. Wasn't *boomtown* either. It was just the leftovers and the seeds of the leftover people—seeds of the exploiters and seeds of the exploited.

My beginnings in Falmouth were extremely humble. Forget what you heard. I know you know my last name; I know it too. But life doesn't always flow the way you think it should flow. And the more I think back on it, the more I realize just how humble these beginnings were. Falmouth wasn't ballin' no more . . . it was futureless. And truthfully I was born into a socioeconomic setup that appeared the same way . . . futureless.

Not long after my birth, my grandmother blessed us with a modest upgrade to our living conditions, and we moved from ground zero at Compound, to 26 Cornwall Street, just a bit farther up the road. This was the first world that I can recall—and is a time I can never forget. Located at 26 Cornwall Street was a tiny little concrete and wooden shack we called home back then. The house felt like it was the size of some of the walk-in closets I see in America today.

The place had only two real rooms: *indoors* and *outdoors*. In truth there were two and a half so-called basic rooms to this shack-house, and those were straining to hold the nine human bodies and nine separate souls that lived under that one shared roof. It was tight. You hearin' me? Extremely. Hell, we were almost packed in as tight as the ancestors were packed in that sardine can that brought us here from across the ocean. This tight little shack-house wasn't much, but it was our own little space in the world.

Of the two and a half rooms that we did have, neither was a kitchen or a bathroom. When I say *two and a half rooms*, I'm not talking bedrooms. I'm talking rooms, period. That's it. Our kitchen was the straight *outdoors*.

Think really deeply on that.

In case you're still not clear on what I'm talking about, let me explain it to you. Our kitchen was a huge blackened pot and makeshift stove where my mom and aunts cooked our dinners and breakfasts over hot coal fires in the blazing Jamaican sun. Rice, beans, or whatever we could manage. It didn't really matter as long as *something* was on that coal-fired stove and we all were eating. And even though there were nine of us, I don't remember going to bed hungry one single night. We ate. And it wasn't going to be any other way. We were all about surviving.

Again, of those two and a half rooms in that wooden shack-house, neither was a bathroom. Feel that. Our bath-room was part of the great outdoors too. That's just how we lived, and how so many of our people still live (and worse) around the world. The showers that we took back then were outside in the brush under a rusty metal spout and Jah's natural sunshine. It was like that. That's all I knew. And with regard to all other toiletry-related business . . . we had what was called a pit-toilet. A pit-toilet, properly defined, is a big-ass hole that's been dug into the ground, with water in the bottom of it and a seat on top—and it doesn't flush. You just climb up and handle your business where a lot of business has already been handled before you. And let me tell you right now, doing your business on a pit-toilet is nothing nice. All of this is most definitely a much nicer process when it's handled indoors on something ceramic that's connected to some pipes that go far, far, far away. I'm just keeping it as real as possible. Indoor plumbing is a beautiful thing! As a matter of fact, it used to be a distinct dream and goal of mine. Some of today's ghetto rap dudes are dreamin' about cars, jewelry, and gold fronts. But wait, wait, wait . . . *I was dreamin' about pipes, man.* Some pipes to carry away my business so I wouldn't have to smell it. Think on that the next time you squat on the throne.

So yeah, we made the point . . . life was on the humble back in Jamaica. We were poor and life was simple, but I'd be lying if I told you that life in Falmouth wasn't good to me. I was no rockstar. I was no reggae prodigy. To the people of my first world, I was just Ky-Mani. Son of Anita. Son of Jamaica. Son of the Caribbean. And many of them knew I was son of Bob Marley. I was a young lad at total peace in an uncomplicated life, and of course, I had no idea about the hurricanes of drama that would ensue when I eventually left this place. Skies were blue. So what did I have to be worried about? Even my meals were the worries of someone else. I was enjoying every little bit of it. It was all still innocent for me. I was still having fun. I was still just a little kid.

Look . . . back when I was young, Falmouth was pure paradise for me. Believe me, I won't front and I can't. It's not in me. The truth is, the way I'm remembering it, my first years on the planet were all bliss. As a little kid or a baby, you don't really think about money or the lack of it as long as there's a bowl of food or a full titty waiting to feed you when you start feelin' the pangs of hunger on the inside.

Life was good—and of course, it's Jamaica, always hot and sunny and cool in the shade. Tropical. That's *always* good. True, it was definitely a slum village, but set on a peaceful countryside, chill and relaxing . . . green grass, goats, cows, and shanty shacks in the sun. It all seems like a calming water-colored painting now. I feel today like there is something mystic about the town. The whole place makes you feel at ease, and not because there's so much blunt in the air—it's just like that. Those were the best days. Irie time.

Being that this was back when I was five and six years old and younger, I can get romantic about the place. I was just a boy enjoying the natural atmosphere and the sweet, sweet ignorance as to how poor we really were. Sometimes the upside of being a little kid is in the not knowing. And I'm telling you, it was this not knowing that helped to make my early years in Jamaica the richest ones to my memory so far. It's when we get a little older and start to *know* that we get it all a little twisted. Your expectations go negative. Your dreams get bruised up. And now you can't even believe in what you used to believe in—'cause you're scared to. True?

But childhood is no limitations. And in this part of my life . . . *no regrets*. I had an amazing childhood. When I reflect on it now, I wouldn't change it. I wouldn't change one thing. In fact, I miss it. I know that sounds crazy to a lot of people, wondering why a fool would miss peein' and cookin' outside in the yard. They're wondering why I would miss living in a Jamaican sun–beaten, hot-ass two-and-half-room shack filled with nine people. But, they're missing the whole thing. They don't get life yet. Not even in the least. They haven't even found a crumb of the clue. I'll explain a little of it to you here.

I do understand that I come from what many might call dirt-poor beginnings, but looking back, in the way I see it, I was a very, very wealthy child. I was a balla-boy. A rich man. *Rich with love.* Rich with the love of family. I was rich in a way that I see so many impoverished and suffering from today. If you don't know anything else, you gotta know this: *money may feed and clothe the body, but the love of family feeds and protects the soul.* It does this in a way that nothing you can buy ever could. I can't keep it more 100 than that. I raise my family by this principle today. I've seen it from both sides, and I'd rather be piss-poor of money than lacking in the love of family any day. And I think on some level we all feel the same way. So yeah . . . realest-town-talk, I lived in an island shack with nine people. Accepted. But listen . . . if I could measure the square footage of that shack-house by the standard of love, I promise you, I grew up in a mansion. I balled.

See, my mother's family is and has always been the most down to Earth, nurturing, caring, and loving of people. They held it down, and they hold it down. Even though every last one of them was penniless, they made the first six years of my young life the best I could have asked for. I was completely surrounded by the light of these people—my grandmother, my aunts, my uncle, the whole community of Falmouth. My life was good. And my life was good because the people I was around were intrinsically good. And I swear this is the substance of what keeps me strong today. It keeps me believing what's possible for people, all around the world. I come from some good stock. Some good genes. Not just from my famous side, but from my mother's side too.

My grandmother is Thelma Henlon, and she ran it, partner. She has always been a deeply spiritual woman who kept it all together for us. She is rich with principle, rich with example. She is the anchor and chief. Despite the size and overpopulation in our house, my grandmother definitely made our shack-house into a home. Our nine-person/

two-and-a-half-room house may have been humble and crowded, but it was always clean, because Thelma kept it that way. And she taught us to do the same. It was always neat and orderly. The Henlon family didn't know it any other way, especially with my grandmother at the helm. Broke in the pocket doesn't mean broken in spirit. This family that Jah blessed me to be a part of was all about it— all about family and all about love. It's what I know, all I know. It taught me, instructed me. It's my foundation.

Coming up in that type of atmosphere did a lot for me. It's like I was growing up in a world of what my dad's lyrics were all about. I was raised under a roof where everybody is One. You know what I mean? Imagine this. In my house? I've never seen a situation where what one has, the other one doesn't . . . or where what one has is too good for the other. I've never witnessed that. I was blessed to never see any kind of segregation like that in my house growing up. I can't say it's like that in every household in Jamaica, but this is what I saw on the daily.

Being in tight quarters like that will force you to either become *family* or despise each other's guts. We could have easily been at each other's throats, but that's not what it was. That's not the example and tone that Thelma Henlon set. We held it down for one another. All I saw was that we were of the same—*One.* We ate from the same pot every night. We drank from the same mug. Everything was shared. Each of those nine hungry mouths got at least *something.* If one of us had a meal, we all had a meal. If one of us had ninety cents, we all had a dime. If one had nine dollars, we all had a dollar. That's how we were with each other. It's been like that from my beginning. That's how I've known it, from my first day.

That's why you can hardly find Ky-Mani today passing a homeless person in the streets without feeling the pain of that, without at least stopping to give *something*. Because of the way I grew up, homelessness is some kind of shit that I just don't even understand. I don't understand how that happens. Every city has hundreds of abandoned buildings and at the same time has thousands of homeless people living on the street. And they're not madmen. These are *people*. So what is this madness all about? We were nine heads in one little house. I guess if I had been raised in another culture, some of our broke-asses would have been homeless and on the street too. It is the shame of us all.

Jamaica is what built the core for me, no matter what was to come later. A person's childhood memories are the concrete foundation of it all. Jamaica represented total freedom to me. I swear the whole thing was like Disney World, compared with where I was headed, and I knew to love it—instinctively. Falmouth was a place where a young boy like myself could run free from sunup to sundown. I could walk the streets near home and all the way uptown without worrying about a thing. I didn't have to worry about anyone harming me. I didn't even have to worry about car traffic since there weren't many of cars in Falmouth back then. It wasn't like nowadays, or like when I moved to America and you had to start being careful of everything. In America you constantly heard about kidnappings, molesters, street drama, and all kinds of dangers that we just didn't hear about in Jamaica, at least not at the time when I was growing up.

On every corner in Jamaica, there was someone to look out for you. It still has that kind of atmosphere now, although with the modern technology and high-speed Internet, it's a little bit more chaotic these days. But in the late 1970s, like I said, I had what I consider full and complete freedom. Even in that crowded two-and-a-half-room shack, I didn't feel claustrophobic—I had the entire city of Falmouth as my playground. I had the run of it. I spent entire days just roaming around from house to house to market to barbershop to soccer field and every point of interest in between. Don't worry; this was all before and after school. I wasn't *that* wild and free. But I was pretty close.

I want to make a point about this again, because I believe that this is what we are straight up missing for these kids today. The point I made earlier about my grandmother was not just true of her; it was something found in the whole of the people in Falmouth. I was living in the type of community where *everybody* was poor in pocket but rich in spirit . . . not just my Henlon family. In a sense, there was a community-family. Hear me on this. Everybody knew my name and exactly who I belonged to. They knew that I was *Anita's boy*. It was just that type of place. There was full protection in this for me, even though there wasn't much to protect me from. In those days long ago, every last community member was an honorary aunt, uncle, or cousin who considered it his or her job and right to have a hand in raising every child in the community. And listen . . . they took this seriously. You could get your ass beaten by someone you didn't well recognize but who knew you and who you belonged to. This was true with no exceptions. These were different times. And the town of Falmouth made no exception with me. They were the definition of community.

Growing up there, I felt like everyone was taking care of me and like everyone was watching me. I wasn't paranoid (I was too young to even know how to be that). It was really true; someone was always watching, just as they should have been. There were no dark corners where I could hide and do dirt without somebody knowing. And there was no time I could find myself in need and not have someone step up to extend some love. That didn't exist there. It was all good. My mom's ears and eyes were in each and every person I would meet, and they knew it was their duty to keep my potential badass under very close observation. You would think that a kid would hate that, but I loved it. Everybody knew each other, and everybody knew me. No strangers. No such thing. I was at peace. And, it felt good. I have no complaints about my childhood. I can puff clouds reminiscing about it all day.

Some of my best memories from this time and place actually came from playing sports. I was a huge soccer fan during that time, and anybody will tell you that I still am to this day. I was completely caught up as a little boy. Absorbed. Obsessed with it you might even say. There was nothing at all better than the competition of sports.

Back then, all I could do was to impatiently wait until school ended so that I could go to The Center with my mom and play soccer. This was *it* for me. I would eat, sleep, and dream soccer. I was so serious with it. On any given Monday through Sunday you'd find me there at The Center or at the park sweating from head to toe. I'd be aggressively kicking a ball around, prepping to become the next Pelé or just looking for an opposing player to put in the dirt so he could ante up and declare me the king. It was all in big fun, and I was all about battle on any level. That truly competitive spirit was a part of my DNA—inherited from my mother as well as my father, who was a big soccer fan too. But I knew that my mom was a famous athlete and champion in the Caribbean, so, of course, I aimed to be no less. I had to show up.

I can remember this one situation like it was yesterday. My mom's a lil' crazy sometimes, but that just makes her who she is. Back at the school in Falmouth, there was a sports competition that we had every so often. They called it Sport Day. I imagine that for the school faculty, it was a little something to help them burn off the extra energy of all those hyper-ass kids. But it was a good thing to keep us fit and active too. I couldn't wait for Sport Day to come around because it would give me a chance to get physical, and sports was just something that came naturally to me. As a little six-year-old lad, I was already known as the fastest boy in my class. And let me tell you, I could *run*. I had the juice, baby. Hands down, I was the champ. Forget everything else you heard. I was shuttin' it down.

And even though Sport Day was supposed to be a chance to just plain out have a little fun, young Ky-Mani didn't listen to this. For young Ky-Mani, Sport Day couldn't be just about fun; it had to be about *battle*. Sport Day was like the frickin' Olympics to me. I was always lookin' to bust some ass, just to let 'em know. Just in case they forgot, and I had to remind 'em. *You couldn't get wit me.* This was COMPETITION. This was serious business. You would have thought I was going to grow up to be the next Carl Lewis or somebody, the fastest sprinter in the world at the time. And Trelawny does have a history of producing world-class sprinters, even today. We take our running seriously. And so did I.

So getting back to the story . . . I was considered the champ, right? Fastest boy in my class. And I was feeling good about that. The whole thing makes me laugh now because I was too young to know the other side of this reality. You know how it goes, when you're the champ—especially a brazen one like I was—you set yourself up. When you're the top tier, you automatically become somebody's aspiration, somebody's target. To call it like it is, you become a marked man. It's the human condition.

I was six years old and nursing a grown man's ego. I needed some kids to eat my dust. And naturally, being the alpha is like a constant invitation for challengers, so I loved it. I loved to serve 'em up a healthy plate of the sad eyes after I totally busted their butts in defeat. If they wanted to race Ky-Mani, I wouldn't deny them the chance. All contenders were welcome. I had that never-back-down attitude even at that young, tender age. The weight of my head was too big for my little underdeveloped neck. Head swellin' outta control! But you know how it goes. Somebody was going to teach me a lesson sooner or later. I just didn't know who it was going to be or where it was going to come from. And it came from the last place I thought it would.

In my class there was one other boy who could kind of give me a good run for it, when he wanted to. He was fast. I'm not going to take anything away from him. He beat me more than once, but in my mind it was always by default. The kid would beat me only when he was running barefoot and I was running in shoes. If we were both running in shoes—on the same even playing field—the kid couldn't win. Period. He couldn't do it.

After a while, I got tired of getting whipped when this boy would kick off his soles and smoke me like he forgot I was the frickin' champion. *Oh really?* I wasn't having that. No sir. Not at all. This was starting to be a problem for my young budding ego. Something had to be done. And quickly.

I had another issue, though. My mother had forbidden me from *walking barefoot, being barefoot,* and *definitely running barefoot.* End of story. She didn't like that. She had her reasons, and she had let it be known on more than one or two occasions how serious she was about this. But there was a conflict, at least for me. This rule was starting to interfere with my objective of maintaining a top-dog status in my class. This kid was trying to lay hands on my shine. C'mon . . . what was I supposed to do?

So I'm watching the calendar. Sport Day was coming up again, and this kid had been beating up on my record— kickin' his shoes off and all that cheatin' shit. Uh-uh. Mom was about to get defied. So I started training and secretly running barefoot. Sorry, Moms. I had to put this kid to rest. Like I said, for young Ky-Mani, this was the frickin' 1981 Olympics. I had to do it. I had to kick those shoes off. *If you weren't tellin', I wasn't tellin'.*

But c'mon . . . really? You know there is only so much that a naïve six-year-old kid can hide from an adult. Kids think they are as slick as the CIA or 007 with their mischievous behavior; they have no idea that to a seasoned adult, they might as well be doing what they're doing in the full light of day. An adult can see you coming before you even form the idea to do what you're gonna do. They've *been there* and *done that* so many times and for so many decades before you were even born, you look like a fool to them. It's a funny thing, because I watch my little ones doing the same thing today and I'm laughing on the inside like . . . *here he comes . . . or here she comes*. Kids, right? Well I was one too.

In my six-year-old mind, for some reason I believe I can keep a secret in Falmouth, Jamaica. Not happenin'. My mother found out I was running barefoot. Of course. But instead of flippin', Anita switched gears on me and started helping me strategizing about how I could beat this boy. She was my continual coach at whatever sport I was into. She didn't give me too much grief for too long about the shoe thing. I guess it was because she knew that I wasn't defying her just to do so. She understood what it was like to not only *want* to win but to *have* to win. So considering all of the above, she's on board now. It's the 1981 Olympics for both of us, and this is serious business. The Caribbean's premier table tennis champ decides that she's going to help me beat my opponent in the upcoming competition. *Okay. Cool.*

I'm trying to remain the undisputed champ. She's coaching me. She's got my ear. We're like Tyson and Cus D'amato. She's laying strategy, and I'm practicing on pure athleticism. Finally, she comes up with an idea for how I can beat him with my *shoes on*. She tells me that she's going to brew this amazing homemade energy drink for me so that I can blaze the trail and leave my competition in ruins. In other words, I'm gonna bust his ass. So I'm all in.

She was feedin' me the whole story, getting me psyched and building my confidence. I know I'm gonna win now. I got Moms in my corner on this too. C'mon, man. I was invincible. This kid thought he was the fastest thing in a 100-yard dash, but I just wasn't built to accept his frame of logic. Plus I was going to add some extra juice to my juice that day. Oh, it was going down. I was about to wrap this dude up in a nice little package send him home cryin' to his momma. You must understand how serious I was. This was Sport Day. *Right?* Right.

D-day 1981. It was finally time. Five-minute warm-up? Check. Hamstring stretches? Check. Game face on? Check. Momma's energy drink? Double check. I had finished breakfast an hour before the competition when my mother called me toward this mug of paste. I took the mug. It smelled a little funny, but I wasn't trippin'. I was all on board with this idea, wanting anything to give me a slight edge. I wanted to win so badly that I just chugged it. I got poured up and took it straight to the head. It had blended oats, milk, peanuts, and all kinds of stuff, but something about it tasted really strange. It tasted disgusting, just as any really good energy drink should, but something was different. It had an odd kick to it. I just couldn't put my finger on the sour flavor of it. It didn't matter. I was ready. I could feel something workin'. I was about to smoke this dude. He would taste defeat today.

I arrived at school that Sport Day ready to put the doubters to rest. Ky-Mani was the champion . . . bar none. I didn't care about any shoes. I was juiced. It was going down. The competition was on. Well, kind of. Ummm.

There was one thing that I hadn't yet realized. What I didn't know was that the major ingredient to Anita's special energy drink was ahhhh, *a Guinness Stout Beer!* She juiced my energy paste with beer! *Whaaat?!* Anita was wilding on me that day! Guinness is no joke for a little virgin six-year-old's bloodstream. My legs were beginning to wobble before I even got to the race. I was so gone. I remember this so vividly, and apparently so do my mom and aunt. They still laugh about this story on the regular.

After all the kids sang the Jamaican national anthem, and after I mostly incoherently mumbled it, it was race time. All seven of the top sprinters walked up to the start line for the 100-yard dash. We were on the line, eager and ready, but I was feeling a little bit outside myself. I was getting hot, and my legs felt like rubber bands. I didn't feel ready. But I didn't know what was going on. So who was I going to tell that I wasn't ready, and what reason was I going to give them?

"On your mark, get ready, get set . . ."

I was so eager that I jumped the line and somebody blew a whistle. *Whoops.* My body and mind just weren't lining up straight. We all had to go back and set the line again. We lined up. I was trying to focus, but it wasn't happening. I was woozy and wobbly. The track was moving back and forth. The sky was starting to spin. *This must be some powerful stuff she gave me.*

They finally started it over.

"On your mark, get set, go."

And that's it. Done. Finished. Okay. That's all I remember. I don't remember starting the race. It's the 100-yard dash! It's the day I had been waiting for. And all I remember is getting halfway down the track and noticing that I was joggin' while all the other kids had finished the frickin' race! I couldn't tell if my shoes were on or off and didn't care. I heard one of the spectators sitting on the wall yell, "Ky-Mani, ah football dem man deh play, dem man deh annu sprinter!" Everybody was laughing and cracking jokes about me. The man was joking that I was made for soccer not for sprinting.

I wobbled over to the side, trying to get right. It wasn't happening. Sometimes after the competitions, they would give the kids a little glucose pack to restore their energy. After the race, I was so woozy that I went over and asked for one. Somebody said, "You don't need no glucose. You didn't even run!" They laughed their asses off. They made fun of me the entire week. They kept saying to me, "How come there were seven people in the race and you come in eighth?" They still clown me on that. I will never forget this day. I came in eighth place in a seven-man race. Have you ever heard of such thing? I was running completely flat-ass drunk at six years old. They stripped my medals from me like my name was Marion Jones. I got completely reduced to just being a legend in my own mind. I was so embarrassed. I not only lost to the dude, I LOST TO EVERYBODY. Thanks to Coach Anita. *Wow.*

Usain Bolt happens to be one of the fastest men in the world today and is from the same area in Trelawny. But somebody tell young Usain that if he sees my momma running up on him talking about her energy drink that'll give him a new world record, he'd better bolt his ass in the other direction. She ain't up to no kind of good, partner. That's my momma, though. She's my rider. For sure. We may have lost the battle, but we were both still determined to win the war.

My Moms is not the typical mother. Not even close. But she was exactly the one I was going to need for the life I was going to have to live. And because we would soon be leaving Jamaica, it was all about to kick into full gear for me. The Jamaican countryside gave me my formative years, as they say. And I think it was these years that give me that quiet inner strength I hold until this day. Energy drink or not, I had to be ready. My first world in Falmouth was coming to an end. These were my memories. I savor every moment of them. My first world was a happy world—a sweet six years before descending into an atmosphere that couldn't be more opposite than the first. But I now had the foundation. My protection. My core. Thelma Henlon and Anita Belnavis made sure I was ready for whatever was to come. And I was definitely going to need that, to survive, on the inside, what was about to happen on the outside.

First Lesson Learned:

"Be rich with
the most important
things in life.
Broke in pocket
does not have to mean
broken in spirit."

2

Ya Fadda Dead

ANITA BELNAVIS WAS NOT ONLY MY MOTHER;
SHE WAS AN INTERNATIONAL CHAMPION. She
was a table tennis champion in the women's competition
division representing Jamaica. This gave her the blessing
and chance to do a lot of world traveling outside of Falmouth.
But back then in Jamaica, among other places, national
athletes weren't making a lot of money like they do now. She
didn't have a glamorous life. No endorsement deals and
such—nothing. It wasn't like that. It was about state pride.
Your country knows you, and they're there to cheer for you;
but the reality was that you go out, you compete, and you
come back to the same shit you left. And that's exactly how
it was for her. It was the times. The mid-1970s.

By the time I was born, my mother had already taken the table tennis scene by storm. For those who don't know, my mom was a top-class contender. That's right, my mom was it. Nuff respect. She was a natural at it, and it was well known that she was one of the very best.

After years of competition and handling her business, and even though it would still be a decade before her sport gained Olympic status, she was eventually crowned the table tennis champion of Jamaica and the entire Caribbean. Jamaican/Caribbean National Women's Table Tennis Champion. She got at 'em real hard, dominating her opponents, mashin' them up. She was that one. She did it. Champion!

She was an international, global competitor. And although she may not have made any money, at the very least, she got a chance to see some of the world as a young woman. She was featured and competing all over the Caribbean, Trinidad . . . all the islands, and especially in Cuba. She even traveled all the way to China for a tournament. And I think she said that China was the only place where she really got her butt consummately whooped. The Chinese handled her and let her know how they got down over there. And if you know anything about the sport, you know how serious they take the table tennis thing in China, Japan, and Korea. They are on that like I was on Sport Day at my Falmouth school. It's extra-serious business. They're not playing with it. It's not Ping-Pong. It's a serious sport with well-conditioned athletes who aggressively go at it with force and skill. Well, Anita took this on and made herself something to hear about. She made some real noise out there.

And like I said earlier, this table tennis thing may not have brought my mom a lot of dough or anything, but it certainly brought her something else that would be life changing. It actually brought her *me*.

Traveling near and far, to and fro, one big tournament took her to Kingston, the capital of Jamaica. She played at the Kingston Arena. Kingston residents came out in droves to see the fast-paced action of the national players, and among the spectators and fans of the sport that day was the one and only Robert Nesta "Bob Tuff Gong" Marley himself. I wish I could have seen this moment. Maybe I could from Heaven. But it was at Kingston Arena where Ky-Mani became a possibility. It was at this tournament that my mother and my father fatefully met for the first time.

My mom was heatin' up the tournament there, doing what she did on the regular. She had just finished a match, crushing her competitor as usual. But after the win, I'm told she went back to the bench to catch her breath and chill out—all the while being scoped out. She had caught my father's eye. While she was sitting there, one her friends came over and said, "Nita. Bob keeps looking at you."

Now, mind you, this is my moms telling me this story, and as she tells it, her friend whispers this in her ear but she really didn't pay it any mind. *No biggie*. But for all that I know, she could have gotten all fussy about it and started straightening her hair and fixing her posture. I laugh about that. You know what I mean? I'm saying, she's telling me this now like she was all cool and laid back about it, but hold on. It's Bob Marley. It's The Gong himself. And he's looking at you. And you're like *whatever*? Maybe. I'm going to respectfully tell it the way she told it to me. She says she was like *whatever*. So, we'll just go with that . . . the whole *no biggie* vibe. Sure.

After the tournament was over, she received some confirmation if there was any doubt as to whether The Gong was becoming a fan. Once again somebody stepped to her and bent her ear. This time she was told that Bob was outside the arena and wanted her to have a word with him for a little while. And I'm guessing she wasn't like *whatever* this time because, well . . . I'm here. And that was the start of that. Or should I say, the start of me? I'm guessing that she went outside, and they both started seeing stars. He probably asked her the general questions that we men do, I'm sure. I know for a fact that he asked where she was from. She, of course, responded, "Falmouth, Trelawny."

I didn't get the whole drawn-out romantic story behind their first meeting, the one with the violins and doves flying overhead. My moms is not the kind who is going to sit around and talk about those things. She's of a different spirit. But I do know that Bob showed up in Falmouth two weeks later looking for her, and that was the start of their romance. And just for the record, and to give Anita her due, my moms was the table tennis champion of all of the Caribbean, so maybe she was in fact all cool and laid back about all this at first. She might've been like, "Bob who? Tell him I'm not signing autographs right now." She was Anita Belnavis. They didn't meet at my dad's concert. They met at *her* show. They were on her block, on her turf at the time. Now that I think about how the story flows, does that make my dad a groupie?

I'm just having a little fun about it. It's all good. It's all about the love anyway, right? That was a special day for Anita and Bob. And obviously that was a special day for me. And that's what Jamaica is for me. Special days, special times, and special memories. That's all I have whenever my mind takes me back to this place and this time in Jamaica. It holds a lot of these beautiful visuals and stories for me. My early childhood holds plenty of memories, but none as treasured as the one I'm about to share. It is the one that is most beautiful to me and still as fresh in my mind as it was the day it was made.

Of the most treasured and vivid memories I have of my early life back in Jamaica is the only vivid memory I have of my father. My one and only living memory of my father, beyond photographs, film clips, and other things, was of a time when he came to visit us in Falmouth. I remember him coming with a friend of his named Sangi, and my elder brother, Stephen. I can see it now.

He pulled onto our grounds in his Land Rover. It was one of those Rovers where you could take the top off of the back. You know, being a boy I pay attention to things like that. Naturally. It's crazy 'cause I can see him now. So clearly. I remember him coming in that truck and picking up me and my moms. We all climbed into that nice truck and rolled out to Nine Miles, where my dad was from. It was good times. There's nothing like seeing the two people who brought you into this world *together*. And it was peaceful. Very. Something about it just makes you feel whole on the inside. Nothing like it. Nothing.

Being a kid, my memory points me to this toy he had brought back from his travels. I know he had just returned from America, and he brought a slingshot back from the States. This was big right there. It wasn't just a regular simple homemade type of slingshot. We were used to the ones where you just had to find a branch on a tree, cut it down, trim it, tape the rubber on either side of the "Y," and you were good to go. But he brought back one that was made of iron. It was made of steel. It was the real deal. You had to slip your hand into it because it had this nice professionally crafted grip. You know, just very well made. It was nice. Best I'd ever seen.

So while we're rolling out and seeing the countryside, I'm having a good time playing with my brother, Stephen. We were getting pretty hyped about this slingshot. I was loving the ride, but I couldn't wait to get to Nine Miles. When we finally get there, we get out of the truck and watch all the adults do what they do . . . but we're really waiting for an opportunity. We had this brand new pro-grade slingshot, and the first thing we wanted to do was test it out.

Finally the adults got situated, and we were freed up to go play. We went deep into the bush in Nine Miles. We were roaming through the jungle-like atmosphere searching for something to shoot at. You know how it is with two boys having fun. I didn't know anything about PETA back then, so I'm sure we were knocking off every bird we could find and bruising up anything bigger. Every animal in the bush was pissed off that day, but we were having a riot of fun. I don't know how much carnage we left behind, but we most definitely enjoyed that slingshot. For sure.

After a while we knew it was getting to be time to head back, so we finally start walking back from the bush. As we're walking, Stephen asks, "Where's the slingshot?"

Whaaaat?! I look back at him. "Why ya asking me?"

He's says, "I'm asking because you had it last."

This was so not the truth, but the slingshot was lost. Gone. Now Stephen is accusing me of losing it. Right? You know how it goes with the whole big brother/little brother hierarchy. He knows he lost it and now he's gotta blame me, just because shit flows downstream. It's a brand new toy, so we both know that this is pretty serious business that it's lost. And it came all the way from America too. Not good.

Stephen figured somebody was going down for this, and it wasn't going to be him. Somebody was going to pay. So he's all ready to frame me. He's straight bullyin'.

I turn to Stephen. "Nah, Stevie, you lost the slingshot."

He shoots back, "Nah you lost the slingshot."

My turn. "Nah, *you* lost the slingshot."

He's about to turn all state's witness on me . . . and he says, "You lost the slingshot and Daddy gon' beat you for it."

Wow, okay. Okay. *So this is how it works, huh, boss?* Now he has to throw in the *beating* part. Nice move.

So, we're walking through all the weeds and grass trying to get back, and I'm carrying all of this in my little mind. Sometimes the anticipation of a coming beating is worse than the real beating when it happens. Meanwhile, in my head, my thoughts are racing. *How could I have lost the slingshot when Stephen is the one who mostly played with it?!* Like I said, he was bullyin', like big brothers do. He was doing most of the shooting, and I was doing most of the watching. But it was still fun at the time.

We're getting closer and closer to the house, and I can now see that my dad is standing in the doorway. I can still see this so clearly, right now. Vividly. It was an old wooden house like ours, with the brick step-up into it. One brick, two brick, then step up into the house. He was standing in the doorway, and I remember just walking up those bricks, ready to take whatever was coming to me. Soldier. Even at that age.

I looked up at him and said, "Daddy, I lost the slingshot."
He looked right down at me. I was ready for it.

Then the most beautiful thing happened. He just smiled the biggest smile at me and burst out laughing. *Whaaat?* In that moment, my first thought was, *Guess I ain't gonna get no beatin'*.

I don't know how Stephen felt about that, but I felt good. It was over. I just turned and walked away. I went back to mind my business. And for some reason, that is the most prominent memory that stays with me. Shortly after that, it happened. Maybe a year and some change after that, my father passed away. It was another one of those moments that is burned into my consciousness. These are my memories.

Robert Nesta Marley
February 6, 1945—May 11, 1981

On the day my father died, I can remember exactly where I was and exactly what I was doing. I'm guessing that wouldn't be too hard to recall because without fail, I was at the same place every evening. At that age, my entire life was dominated by the one thing that I loved the most—soccer. So, I was at the park in the middle of a game when a man approached me. I don't remember who the guy was or even if I knew him, but I definitely remember what he said. "Your mom wants you to come home *now*."

Of course, I'm in the middle of doing what I love to do most, and like any child, I'm not ready to hear that playtime is over. So I start questioning him.

"What for?" I ask.

The guy answered me saying, "I don't know, but she says she need you to come home right *now.*"

Really?

The whole thing was strange to me. I had never been called home from the park. Never. It was Falmouth. So I was in a place where when I finished playing, pretty much on my own time, I'd go home. That's just the way it was. No pressure. No worries. Everything was easy and laid back. But nothing was easy and laid back about this. Something was up.

So, of course, my mind is starting to race, trying to figure out what the deal is. But after a second, I thought, *Okay. That's not a problem.* And I picked up my ball and started the walk toward home.

As I walked home from the park, I bopped around down the street still kind of playing around with my ball. I get closer and closer. Where we lived was like a one-lane road. It was like a little alley and then the row of structures start. It's a tenement setup, almost. On our row, you had the barbershop and then somebody in the first lil' house. Our house was the second house. As I pass the little cabin-like buildings, I'm still thinking to myself, *What could be so urgent that I have to stop playing soccer?* I remember walking, looking around—something wasn't normal. I stepped up to my house, and there was nobody there. *Well, okay. Where is she? I wonder.*

I step outside. I start walking again, and it's really starting to get odd 'cause I'm not seeing the usual activities that go on outside with neighbors and whatnot. I keep heading down the row of structures looking for signs of life. Finally, I find her. I actually find her two more houses down at a friend's house. Not only is she there, it seems like the entire village is there. I later find out that they were all there because this house had a little television setup and hardly anyone had any television of any sort for the one Jamaican TV station. But two houses down we had a friend who was blessed like that. I peep in; the little house is full.

I step up into the house with my soccer ball on my hip, still trying to catch on to what I'm seeing in front of me. Everybody's gathered around the TV. They're just completely fixated on it. I'm standing there, and I remember the vibe was just weird, you know? In my young lifetime, I had never felt this vibe before, and all my people are in one place all at the same time. Something ain't sittin' right. Their faces looked drained. There was no conversation. None of the kids were running around or playing. Everybody was just sitting there—frozen, stunned, zombied.

I have no reference point for what I'm seeing, so I then go and stand in the middle of the group, just looking at 'em. One by one, they all awaken from their daze and start looking up at me. Now I'm really taken aback. Nobody is speaking. Nobody is acknowledging me. I'm not liking the look on their faces—at all. And then finally someone said something. Finally.

It was a female but it wasn't my mom. It was a young girl. She looked up at me, breaking the thickening drone of the TV chatter and said straight up, "Ya fadda dead."

Silence.

In an instant I became like the zombies that I didn't understand. Shocked. A lump of feelings pushed up from within me like an earthquake inside. Shattering everything.

No words. I didn't know what this was. I didn't know what any of this was. But I did. On some level, I did. Her words were stuck in a loop inside of my head now. A loop that would never leave.

I turned and ran out of the house. I was too young to know that this wasn't the type of danger you could escape from—with all the might and speed in my legs, I couldn't run from it. It was everywhere I turned. The park, the barbershop, school, the neighbors' houses. It was everywhere. And it never ceased being everywhere, ever since that day. So huge, it hung in the skies. Reality. The reality of what she said. To me.

The impact of it hit me hard. It was crazy. It was as if I knew in that moment that I was just cheated out of a lifetime. I was just cheated out of a father—an injustice never to be rectified.

I had my moment. I definitely had my moment.

"Ya fadda dead."

Words never forgotten. Never. They ring as clear as any voice I hear today.

The young girl who broke the silence wasn't being insensitive by the bluntness of her words. At best, she was only a couple of years older than I was. And that was the only way she knew how to express what had happened. Everyone was crying or beginning to . . . including her. And no one else was volunteering to say anything. I guess they were choked with the shock and grief of it all. Like I became. The little girl was the only one who could find the strength to say it. And so she did.

It was done. That was that. You just go on.

We're from nothing, you know. Like I told you, nine of us were living in that two-and-a-half-room house with a makeshift outdoor kitchen that we shared with everybody else who lived in the yard—and the bathroom was the same situation. Same thing. When you live like this, there's a lot you just learn to accept. You have to. Anything else will drive you crazy if you allow it. Accept. And go on.

I can remember now coming up to the funeral ceremony—the wound still fresh—the pain still present. But it was time for that whole part of it to go down. The part that's extremely hard for me to talk about. It's hard to speak about it because it kills me on the inside until this very day, all these years later. The funeral incident stays fresh and lingers, because I didn't get a chance to attend my father's funeral. My own father. That shit devastates me until this very day.

Some might ask if it was a political thing with all of the petty dramatics going on among the adults, but I don't know and I can't say. All that I can say with definiteness is that it shouldn't have happened like that for me. I was just a child. A little boy, broken up over his father's passing. There ain't no politics in that. Period.

For all my time lived until now, I've tried not to think about these things and just let it lay. I really do. But they stay with me. And I find that willfully not thinking about it and willfully not talking about it doesn't mean that the pain ever stops burning. Even as I write about it now, it is fresh. But it's just the way it is.

Although the spirit was no longer there with that body, it was the last opportunity I would ever get to see this man physically. Ever. That's it. For life. No going back. No undoing. Swallow. Accept. Burn. Go on.

He was given a state funeral. It was the talk of the town. The talk of the island. My mother and I didn't share many words about it, at least not that I remember. I just remember her asking me if I wanted to go to the funeral. I told her, "Yeah, I wanna go."

I know she was trying to find a ride and gonna put in a call to Kingston to see if they would send somebody to come get me. But it didn't happen. No one came. No one. I remember waiting the entire day. It never happened. I ended up listening to my father's funeral and eulogy on the radio. The *radio*.

It was an important moment. The fact that our condition was what it was, how we were living with nothing and without means, should have been considered. It wasn't like people didn't know about it. People definitely knew whose child I was and where I lived and everything else. This was no secret. And just the fact that it wasn't secured that I made it to my own father's funeral was, to me, a slap in the face. It's fresh. It set the tone that I've been feeling since that day.

Remembering, I think I listened to a good majority of it until . . . I guess . . . I just couldn't take it anymore. At the top of my yard, there was the barbershop where they had the radio playing loudly. They were playing the live broadcast of the funeral. It was all over the island. This was a national event. I slowly walked into the barbershop to listen. I don't know what the people who were there were thinking of me, or the situation with me being The Gong's child and forced to listen to my father's funeral with them. I was too young to care about that. All I could think about was him. Just him.

I listened to a little bit of it, then I'd go outside for a little bit and have my moment—then I'd go back in and listen to some more. All this is happening when I'm five years old.

My moms told me that my father had been shopping for property in Falmouth. He was buying a house for us. But he became ill with cancer, and things quickly fell apart. The vultures descended, as they do, to help him fall. My mom also told me that she heard that the wife of my father, Rita Marley, said, "All of Bob's dutty baby's mothers and bastard children will suffer." Quote. Unquote. *Wow.* And so it was.

That would be the beginning to everything else that was to come. And for a long time, that meant nothing good. That started the struggle, and it's been an uphill battle ever since. It was all about to define who I would become. That moment would resonate. It would resonate for many years to come.

Second Lesson Learned:

"When the flesh of a loved one leaves you, know that you will never be alone as long as the spirit of their heart walks within you. A million earthly enemies can stand against you, but when one heavenly friend stands with you, you will prevail again and again. Push on."

3

Mother's Milk

I CAN'T CREDIT MY MOTHER WITH ALL OF WHO I AM TODAY. I can't do this because I can't say that I'm *all* good. But for the great majority of me that is good, I credit my mother with 100 percent of every drop of it. If you were to ask me who my mother was and is for me, I could only cheat you with words that were not enough to describe her. You might be satisfied with my answer, but I wouldn't be—because I would know. I would know that my words were not serving her the smallest bit of justice.

My mom? For me? She's my mother . . . my friend . . . my rock . . . my hero. And if you don't have one like that, I feel deeply for you. I don't know where I'd be without mine. I don't even want to think about that. But I for damned sure wouldn't be here with you right now. I might be dead, in prison, or plotting to rob you and therefore on my way to prison. I would be in complete darkness—with no hand to pull me out. That's what this woman has meant for me.

There's nothing weak about my mother. She's a woman. One hundred percent so. But even from a man's point of view, when I think of her, all I can think about is the idea, image, and example of *strength* itself. If you look up *strength* on Wikipedia, it is this woman's photograph that you should see. Yeah, the mother's milk I got was a special, special brew.

As a young lad, I was fed no stories of falsehood and fantasy. My bedtime stories weren't *The Lady in the Shoe* or *The Cow Jumped over the Moon*. No, Anita wasn't for that. She wasn't for reading me fairy tales. No fables. No nursery rhymes. My mom read stories to me about iconic revolutionary figures like Steven Biko, Che' Guevara, Nelson Mandela, and Malcolm X or stories about the Fidel Castro movement. These were my bedtime stories. No fables. No fake heroes. Real life. Biographies. She gave me real heroes that were real people.

She nurtured me with stories that were related to life in a way that bettered life. She nurtured me with stories that were part of a movement that changed humanity or that changed a nation. She nurtured me with stories about people who meant something to millions of other people, affecting their lives and improving the quality of their lives. My mom was and is no joke. Not in the least. I love Anita.

It was those kinds of teachings that helped mold and shape the character that I would eventually grow into and that still contribute to the person that I am becoming today. It was a powerful seed. I was being told stories that made me begin to look up to a certain kind of person with a certain kind of mentality that is not just for *self* but for the *greater good*. So I started researching these people and looking into their backgrounds and humble beginnings, searching for what motivated them. I think those early teachings caused me to inquire more and want to know more about the Great Ones of life. Feel my passion on this.

We didn't have a TV back in Jamaica. It wasn't like I could sit and watch TV for hours and euthanize my mind like our children do today by the millions. There was no false hero to idolize or reason to want to be these false, empty, zero-dimensional characters you see today on our televisions. It was the stories that my mom told me about Che' Guevara, about the revolution in Cuba, about Steven Biko—freedom fighters. She taught me that the struggles of African peoples everywhere was my struggle. So at a very young age, I wanted to be like these kinds of people. I wanted to be the revolutionary who was going to stand up against the system, for the people. I wanted to be a Babylon rebel. These heroes fascinated me as a child. I wasn't watching Captain America or Superman. I didn't have that channel. Couldn't tune in. Thank Jah Almighty. I had *real* heroes who gave me substance. And my mom is obviously and honestly the biggest of 'em all.

This woman nurtured my body in health, and she sculpted my mind with consciousness. She was no ordinary mother to me. And she couldn't afford to be. She gave me this mind-set of "militant determination." Survival. She taught me to never back down from anything. Stand up. Fight. And as a result, I stand up for mine no matter what the consequence is. Win, lose, or draw. That's been instilled in me since birth. She taught me that I had the strength to face anything that came my way. Anything. She was hardcore about it. She was raw about it. No watering down, no sugarcoating for taste. It was pure and concentrated—and therefore effective.

I think that once my father passed away, she knew she was going to have to feed me the strength that I would not receive from him as a boy or young man coming of age. She did that. She did it the best way she knew how. And let me tell you . . . as straight as I can . . . if there is one gift that my father gave me that I will love him eternally for, it is the gift of my mother, the soil in which he placed the seed of me. She was a nutrient-rich soil from which I drew strength. She molded me and shaped me into the man that I am today.

Nothing less than extraordinary, this woman is special to me. And I don't want you to think that my mom dressed in military fatigues and boots and marched me off to school in a beret. It wasn't like that. True, she had to be my father and fill in the gap, but she was definitely still my mother too. I still knew she was my moms. Anita was still the same person who brushed my hair in the morning, lotioned me up, got me dressed, cooked my food, and nurtured to me. All of that side of my mom was there too. But Anita wasn't the type to be all mushy-mushy with you, at least not with me. If I were a girl, maybe she would have been different. But I can tell you, I didn't feel as though I was lacking in one way or the other. She gave all that she had to me. Female nurturance. Male guidance. I mean there was only so much that a young single black female could do for her child-son in the socio-economic ghetto circumstances that were our reality, but she did all that she could. She didn't slack. It's never easy without a father around to make a boy a man. But she did the very best that she could . . . and then some. And what else can you ask for? Anita, handled that shit, hands down. I watched her. Respect.

My grandmother and aunts were also around. They too made sure that I wasn't lacking for anything. They gave a *lot* of love and nurturance to me growing up—all that they could. We were all living together in the same place. I was surrounded by family. I had Aunt Angela, Aunt Barbara, Aunt Holly, Uncle B, my cousins—Ron, Ryan, Ayesha Benjamin, Atari David Bigby (who now plays safety for the Green Bay Packers) . . . I had a whole clan.

My beloved grandmother, Thelma Henlon, definitely put her stamp on me. I've always been very close to my grandmother. I was close to both my grandmothers, but I was raised by my mother's side of the family, so my mother's mother and I were especially close. Inside and out, she is the most beautiful person in the world to me. I am not mindlessly speaking these words because she is my grandmother; she is the sweetest person one could meet. I've watched this woman feed crackheads who were homeless in our neighborhood when we ourselves barely had enough. This is the type of woman she is. So when I say she is the sweetest person and the most beautiful person in the world to me, I mean that. I never met Mother Teresa, but I met Thelma Henlon. My grandmother is a person you want to be around. And if you meet her, I definitely think you'll say the same thing because she's just naturally that type of person. Just her being nearby makes you feel better.

I guess you could say that if there was any of that softer side that I may have missed from my mom, I definitely got that filled in full by my grandma. That was just who she was to me. When I really, really needed that softer side, I could always look to her. In her eyes, I could do no wrong. She could see the love in me . . . and not judge me for my temporary means of finding myself—finding the love that she sees. I was the first grandchild, so it was just that way. And from that time until now, she has always been that person . . . the example of a Christian, and a die-hard Christian at that.

Every Sunday my grandma attends church. Without fail. I remember as a young boy, every Sunday I would want to go to church with my grandma just to be with her, for real. So not only was I raised Rastafari, I was raised under

Christianity, which is really one and the same. I would definitely say that if there was any other person who put a stamp on my life other than my mom and my dad, it would truly be Grandma Thelma Henlon. Respect.

Like I have said, despite our circumstances, my mom gave me an amazing childhood. It was all love. My mom and I have always had a special connection, like brother and sister. I was lucky. Really lucky. Yeah, she was Mom, no doubt about that, but even in the midst of all that, there was something special about our relationship. My mom taught me about *everything*! Even when it came to playing soccer, it was my mom who coached me.

In Jamaica everybody played soccer. And with Anita Belnavis being a pro-ranked athlete, she was able to handle herself skillfully too. I had an uncle, Richard Henlon, who was a great soccer player, and he would give me some pointers as well. He played center-forward for the national Jamaican team. But it was my mom who would taught me how to shift, how to get rid of a defender, how to body rock (that is, how to fake out the opponent by movin' my body without moving my foot). I can still hear her telling me, "Use the left foot. Use the weaker foot." There's no getting better than that. I love my mom. It was these moments . . . her stepping in to help me learn how to control the ball in my chest, how to hit the ball . . . these moments that tremendously helped fill in the hole of not having a father present. The Gong was a great soccer player himself . . . my father.

But it fell to Anita to teach me about soccer, and she did, down to the details of body shifting with the ball while still moving forward without changing stride. That's how deep she was with it. Even when I started playing American football, decked out in shoulder pads, a helmet, and cleats, she would say, "Listen, it's just like soccer. You're gonna get that defender in front of you the same way." It was like that. That's how she was. Not scared to parent me in any way. She was coaching me.

I was a star athlete in high school. And it was definitely a lot of her teachings that helped me put a lot of people on their asses. Whatever she would tell me, I would go out there and try it. It worked—and worked well. I wasn't drinking any more of her energy drinks, but the rest, I tried. The rest worked. And that's how we did it. She was involved. She was interested. She was creative. We were a unit. I had her back, and she had mine.

You know how when you're a little kid and you're sitting there, don't wanna eat 'cause something doesn't look right or something doesn't smell right, or its too pasty or too lumpy, or its too saucy? (You know the drama around kids and eating.) And the real reason you're giving your parents drama is because you want to go back outside and play. Remember those days? Well, my mom always knew just the right way to handle this situation with me. She wouldn't get upset or try to force me to eat. She found a way to make eating fun for me. She got creative with it.

Here's an example of how absolutely dope this woman was and still is. When I would act like I wasn't hungry and wouldn't eat, she would pretend like she was commentating a soccer game between my older brothers and me. She'd start, "Marley passed the ball to Stephen. Stephen passes it back to Ky-Mani. Ky-Mani breaks one, breaks two. He shoots, he scores, and the crowd goes wild! Yeah!" Maaaaaaan . . . that shit got me so excited. I would eat all my food right then and there and then get right back out there on the field playing. That's love, right there. In action.

My mom made sure I stayed healthy and strong in mind, body, and spirit. Even though we were poor, she did her best to make me feel like I wasn't lacking anything. I'm drilling this point deep because I want you to walk away with something. By now, there is no question as to how I view this woman and no wondering how or why I see this woman as the hero of my life. No mystery. Hands down, *she's the best*. My mother was there for me in a way that I could never doubt, even if I got pissed and tried. Not all children are that lucky. Many live their lives wondering if their parents really love them or want them or value them—and they sit there sometimes with these questions eating away at their little souls. Anita gave me nothing but clarity. I knew who was in my corner. And right now I'm trying to make it clear who my mother was for me so that all the other single moms struggling out there, trying to fig-ure out how you are going to do this thing and make it through, can see that it's possible. I want you to see the strength of my momma and see that it can be done under any circumstances. She was forced to be two parents in one. And, again, my mother handled that. She did it. And I love her till this day for it.

When my father died, my mom and I didn't speak much about the pain or the negative of it. In some ways that was good, and in some ways, bad. But when your mind is stuck on survival, it just kind of happens like that. There's not a lot of time to cry. I'm the kind of person who could be going through hell and you'd never know it. It won't show it. I keep a smile on my face at least fourteen hours out of the day, 'cause I'd be lying if I said twenty-four. I've always been like that. I've been more like the type of person who would take on other people's problems first than to stress people with my own. I'd just rather deal with it on my own. You have your share; I have mine. And that was the kind of the vibe we had around the pain and loss of my father. We just didn't talk much about it. We both dealt with it internally in our own way.

In her way, I know she grieved. Back then she was more of the mind of militancy. She had a revolutionary mind-set. She had a soldier's mind-set. And when a soldier falls next to you, you march on toward the goal, taking that spirit with you. She was the person who even in the middle of crisis, even if she were to have her own emotional episodes of breaking down, wasn't going to break down in front of me.

She was about staying strong and moving forward under all circumstances. That's what she wanted to project to me as a lesson and a way of approaching life. Lesson received.

I do remember, though, some shared moments we had around the death of my father. Some very unorthodox moments. Odd things happened around the time of my father's funeral. I guess it's not completely right for me to say *odd*. It wouldn't be odd to some people, and it does happen to a lot of people after they've lost someone. But to others—those who don't know anything about, or who have never had any experience with, the spiritual realm of things—this type of thing would probably seem odd.

To put this in perspective, I should start by explaining that my mom had a regular night that she would go out with a girlfriend, teammate, or other friend. We lived in the country, so they walked everywhere they went. They would sometimes walk through areas where there was no moonlight due to foliage and trees. And there were no city lights, so you couldn't see two steps in front of you in most areas.

So at times when my mom would come in from being out, it would be too late for her friend to walk home. Whichever friend she went out with would just stay over. And when this happened, we would all sleep in the same bed together. It had become a routine. They'd just move me to the middle of the bed and fall asleep on either side of me till the morning. I was used to this. I was used to waking up in the middle of the night sandwiched between two warm bodies.

However, on one of these regular late nights, a couple of days after my father's services, I was home with my mother, who had returned home from having stepped out earlier. I remember this one night in particular because my mom was fast asleep by the time I crawled into the bed. And as I'm lying there in the bed sleeping . . . and I'm pretty far gone by now . . . I kinda curled up a bit and stuck my knee out. As soon as I did this, I had the clear sensation of another knee touchin' my knee. *Okay, no problem,* I think. *It's a knee. There are always extra knees and elbows in our bed.* So without fully opening my eyes, I said to my mother (and I remember this vividly): "Mommy . . . how much of us are in the bed?"

And she responded, "Two. Just me and you."

I said, "Okay," and at this point, I went back to sleep.

So, I'm lying there, falling asleep, and after a while I feel the same thing again. Something came out and touched me from the other side. That is, something kind of pushed on me, you know? So I asked again. "Mommy . . . how much of us are in the bed?"

And she replied, "Two."

I said, "Are you sure you didn't bring Pauline home with you?"

She answered, "No, it's just me and you in the bed."

Then she asked, "Why?"

I said, "Because somethin' keeps touchin' me. Somethin' touched me."

She was quiet for a minute before she finally said, "It's just me and you in the bed."

That was it. I let it go. I went back to sleep.

When we woke up the next morning, my mom finally said, "Come here." She sat me down as if for a chat . . . to tell me something. She looked into my eyes and said, "Listen, it was more than the two of us in the bed."

She went on to explain that after I had awakened her that last time, asking her the question, "How much of us are in the bed?" she felt a presence herself. She said she felt the end of the bed sink in like somebody sat down on it. She told me that her eyes were open, but when she tried to look, she couldn't move or turn her head. She then added that she heard what sounded like someone walking and the back of his slippers dragging on the floor. She heard the feet drag all the way through the house until she finally heard the door open and shut. After this, she said she was then able to look up. But by this time she didn't see anything. It was good to know I wasn't alone and going crazy about this.

I don't know how many times something like that had happened to my mother, but it was my first experience with anything like that. For a lot of people who have lost loved ones and who had similar experiences, they can relate and know it's a real thing. For me, it would turn out to be the first of many times that I would have experiences like that. On the real, that moment to me was another defining moment in my life. Because, for whatever reason that I took it the way I took it at that age, for me, that was him. It was my father. And when my mom woke up and confirmed it for me, after it happened twice, I knew what it was. I was just like, *Okay. Well he come and visit me.*

And we just went on.

Third Lesson Learned:

"*Love doesn't give up. It fills what is empty. It strengthens what is weakened. It creates what is not there. It even brings back to life what has passed away. Love is the opposite of the impossible.*"

4

Broken Promised Land

WHEN I HEARD ABOUT THE POSSIBILITY OF MOVING TO AMERICA, I WAS EXCITED. But I swear, after the first morning I opened my eyes in this new promised-land, I would have run all the way back to Jamaica if they had built a bridge that long. 26 Cornwall Street was a million miles away, and getting farther.

Leaving Jamaica became a possibility through my grandmother. My grandmother was a nurse in Jamaica, and her mother, my great grandmother, lived in America. Specifically, she lived in Miami. She had gotten her papers and said, "We think America is where you're gonna find your pot of gold." So she decided she was going to file for her children and, of course, her grandchildren. Next thing you knew, we were all going to move up to try for a better life. To uplift. She truly believed that America was where we were all going to rise and enjoy a better life.

Back in Jamaica, America was talked about with the highest regard. We were told, "This is the place where all your dreams come true when you get there." I remember when my grandmother used to return to Jamaica after visiting the States. She would give us a U.S. dollar, and we would take it to the shop and get eight Jamaican dollars back in exchange. Oh, we loved that. So, naturally, in our minds, we thought that America was the place to be. We knew nothing but all *good*. And not to mention, I couldn't forget that this was the place from which my dad had brought that pro-grip slingshot. That was proof enough right there. America was *the bizness*! Everything was better in America.

When it was time to leave Jamaica, there was big, big excitement. Just the thought of it was exciting. My aunts and my cousins had already made the transition. They had left before my mom and I. And honestly, that kind of made me sad because I had grown up with them and they were part of my life each and every day. I had never had to be without them before. I was missing them, especially my little cousin. They were my little playmates, so when they left Jamaica, home felt kind of empty and lifeless. I just wasn't used to that. I stayed sad about it for a while. My mom and I were left behind for about two months before we could go.

While we were still in Jamaica, my little cousin would call us from America. It was like torture. My mom and I would go to the pay phone and have to hear from everyone. It was good to hear from them, but it was bad that we weren't there with them. Ayesha was my girl cousin, and I can still remember the first time I talked to her when they got to America. It was all excitement. She told me that she was in the kitchen playing dolly house. And I thought, *Wow, a kitchen.*

So I started building this concept in my head of the exact layout of the house. I had it all mapped out even though I'd never been there. I pictured a house with a white exterior and a clean and spacious interior. Back in Jamaica, of course, we were still cooking outside on a coal stove and showering outside with no hot water. In fact, our shower was just a pipe surrounded by zinc and a slab of concrete. That's where I'm used to showering, so just hearing about the luxuries in America is blowing my little mind. I'm hearing about *indoor* showers and *indoor* kitchens. *Whoa.* I was ready to roll out *now.*

At this point, I'm so looking forward to this moment that it couldn't get here fast enough. Forget the INS paperwork; I was ready to be on some straight Elian Gonzalez type of shit. I was ready to go. This was big stuff—the biggest good thing to happen to me. Right? So I'm extra anxious. You know how kids are when they are looking forward to something. And we were talking about indoor plumbing, partner. My dreams were *already* coming true.

The day finally arrived when we got the green light to roll out. And the good thing about not having anything is that you don't have a lot to pack. We could just pick up and go. I can remember being on the plane. It was nighttime, and we had just flown over the Gulf. The flight wasn't that long, of course, but this was all such a big deal to me. I'm six or seven years old and on an airplane. That was already some major stuntin' for me. Major. And as I looked outside of the window, I was in complete awe. It was an incredible sight—a work of art. We were coming in over Miami as the plane was descending, and it was just beautiful. I was looking out over what seemed like a million lights, glistening, dancing, and putting on a show. It was as if the stars had all fallen to Earth. I was awestruck. I was thinking to myself, *Wow, this place is much more beautiful than I thought.* From 15,000 feet and descending, it looked like everything a paradise should be. It was all making sense. It looked perfect.

Once we landed, we deplaned and found a cab. It was completely dark outside, definitely the middle of the night. We rode in the cab, taking in the night sights. It was dark, but I could still see a little. This place was amazing. Everywhere I looked, amazing. It was nothing like the countryside of Falmouth.

We finally arrived at my grandma's house. We hopped out and went into the little house. I was extremely happy to see everybody. I had arrived. Finally. No more pay phone updates. I was in America. There were hugs, kisses, and a mood of celebration, of course. It was a good time. Finally, I took a look around the house. The place was, of course, not really what I was envisioning. Not large, not spacious—definitely not—but it was still nice, or so I think.

The first thing I did was take a shower—*indoors*. And there was some hot water too. It was the best thing ever. The best. After that shower, I thought to myself, *Maybe this America thing is alright, you know?*

I'm yet to see the reality of what's really about to hit, so for the moment, I was enjoying it. I couldn't wait to see it in the daytime; I thought it would probably be even more beautiful than at night. We went to bed that night with no problems. Everybody sleeps well after a warm shower.

Finally the sun rises, and the glow of sunshine streams into the house. I wake up. It wasn't a dream. I am still here. *I'm in America!* I climb out of bed. My vision is still adjusting to the full light of day as my eyes take in the full view around me. Left, right, front, back—the full 360. The brightness in my eyes starts to grow darker and darker as I'm seeing what I am seeing. I'm seeing the house in the light now.

You have to understand. I've come to America, right? And I'm discovering that the wooden house that I lived in back in Jamaica was a better house than the wooden house I'm standing in right now. It was in better condition. And this was all becoming clear now as I saw the house in the full light of day. Just that fact alone took me totally by surprise, because clearly it was supposed to be the other way around. I mean, other than the perk of having the kitchen inside of the house, which at that point really didn't make any sense because the little kitchen was so tiny, I wasn't seeing the upgrade. My cousin said she was playing dolly house *in* the kitchen. She didn't say it *was* the kitchen.

Now the reality was slowly setting in that we were actually all back in a two-and-a-half-room house, all nine of us. But this is a smaller two-bedroom house than the little two-and-a-half-room shack on the Jamaican countryside. I know that's hard to believe, and it was hard for me to believe too. It didn't seem like we got an upgrade; it seemed like we moved to the side and backward a little.

So imagine it. All nine of us in a smaller dwelling. It was me, my mom, my two aunts, my grandma, my uncle, and the whole crew of cousins. We have the pullout couch in the living room and another twin bed on the wall. It was like some real refugee living. For me it was a complete disappointment; it wasn't even close to the image of what I had built up in my mind. The house wasn't a fraction of what I pictured. There was no clear upgrade. But I really don't know if it was all of this that disappointed me so much. Indoors was what it was. We were used to tight living. It was family. I could adjust my expectations. It was what I saw when I stepped outside that was decimating.

Once outside, I'm hit by another reality that I wasn't ready for. Not . . . at . . . all. I go and stand on our stoop. I do another 360. I'm looking outside directly across from my house and see nothing but bushes, old abandoned cars without tires, busted windows, and spray paint graffiti everywhere. *Wow. Guess I won't be playing soccer out there.* I look toward the same direction right across the street and I'm seeing crackheads smoking crack right in front of me—just *steps away.*

As a child at this point, I don't know what they're smokin' but I know it ain't weed; I knew what weed looked and smelled like. Whatever they're smokin' is some other shit. I look up and down the block and see these different kinds of people that I've never been exposed to before. As I look around this neighborhood, a newly transplanted little kid, I think, *What. The. Hell. Is. This?* That's the exact feeling I had at that moment. To say that I was utterly disappointed would be the understatement of the century. In this new land, I was slowly realizing that I was waking up from a dream into what was shaping up to be a nightmare.

So for me, the whole idea of coming to America was no longer. It was done. I can remember waking up that morning and wanting to go back to Jamaica—immediately. Point blank. This was not *the bizness* at all. Lemme tell you. Other than having my family there, united again, this wasn't it. This ain't feelin' good. Not one bit. On top of that, there were no parks nearby, I knew absolutely nobody in the neighborhood, and the place was just flat-out violent. My whole program was yanked, and for this? I had the good life back in Falmouth. I can pass on this America shit. Young Ky-Mani was ready to mash out, bounce, adios. I was ready to do the Elian Gonzalez thing back in the other direction.

I remember the first week we were there; the cops were in my neighborhood damn near every other day. Faithfully. Noisy, aggressive, arrogant assholes. I remember my first experience during the same week. I was just standing at the gate of the yard, crackheads across the street doing what they do plus the dudes on the corner doing their dealing. I remember this too, vividly. All of a sudden a flower-van slowly approached from down the street. The back opens and a whole bunch of police jump out. And at that time, at that age, I didn't know what was going on 'cause all I saw were people jumping out with full black masks and guns. I'm sitting there watching this whole thing go down in front of me, wondering, *What's this?* This was a whole different cycle of life than what I had been exposed to.

In Jamaica, I lived in the country and there weren't a lot of killings. I mean, you just didn't get a lot of that. You would hear of people beating other people or fighting but it wasn't violent *like this*. And I most definitely wasn't used to the crackheads wildin' on the block or police in ski masks jumping into the street like a paramilitary unit. Welcome to America. *Wow*. It was a reality check. And there was no turning back at this point, so we had to simply adjust and go on.

This board-house we moved into was the worst house in a ten-block radius. We had the only wooden house for blocks around. Everyone else's was stone or brick. Our kitchen was indoors, but was it? We would be standing in this little-bitty-ass kitchen with a big frickin' hole in the wood. I could stand in the kitchen and look through the wood and be looking outside. It was like that. And when winter time came, all that cool air would blow right on through, and there was nothing you could do but try to put something up to block the air. I was coming into that reality. But what was I going to do? As a kid, you just go where you go.

After a while, you kind of naturally settle in and get acclimated, gaining a little more of a grip on what's happening around you. Time starts to give you an understanding of your environment and surroundings. So, after some days passed, I started taking it as it comes. What's the use of getting all bent out of shape? We were here. And we were not leaving.

I remember being this little child and having my first experience as far as gunplay is concerned. I was out in my yard behind a gate. Listen closely: I said *behind a gate*. It wasn't the freedom of Falmouth anymore. I didn't know anything about gate life. I went from a free-roaming kid to a prisoner. I couldn't tell if the gate was locking me in or locking them out. Really it did neither. If you lived in this neighborhood, you were going to be touched by it in some way. And on this day, that little gate definitely wasn't keeping the neighborhood out.

I remember standing out there in the yard. Just another beautiful day in Liberty City, Miami. All of a sudden two of my new neighbors begin to argue. One lived in front of me and the other lived behind me on another street. They're having this argument while each of them was still on his own street. But everything was so packed together in the city layout they might as well had been on the same one. One neighbor was sitting in his car, with the car door open. The other neighbor is standing there in the street. The argument is brewing. As a matter of fact, it's beginning to rage. I could feel the tension expanding in the air.

I'm just sitting there, six years old, watching and listening to them go at it. And the next thing I know, the words going back and forth are replaced by bullets whizzing back and forth. *Pop, pop, pop, pop!* This is not TV. This is not a movie. And for damned sure, it is not a cartoon.

I'm sitting there watching a shoot-out take place right in front of me, and I haven't moved yet. My head is bopping back and forth, watching the action like a spectator at Wimbledon. Shots from the front, shots from the back, answering each other. I don't know where my mother is, or uncle, or grandmother, but I know where I am. I'm watching one dude with a rifle shoot through my yard at the next dude who's standing up at the back fence and shootin' back at him. I'm just posted on the yard watching this like it's normal, not knowing how normal it was going to be. But it definitely never came into my mind the danger that I could possibly be in. I had never seen this before. It was something new. Like I said . . . if this is the American Dream, I wanted somebody to wake me the hell up.

Fourth Lesson Learned:

"No matter the pitch, no matter the presentation, no matter the promise . . . always read the fine print."

Very Rude Boy
(Unnecessary Badness)

MAYBE THAT FIRST IMAGE OF MY NEIGHBORS TRYING TO BLAST EACH OTHER'S HEADS OFF THE FUCKIN' HINGES LEFT A LASTING IMPRESSION ON ME. There were real live rounds flying back and forth through the gates of my front yard. And when this type of shit is whizzing past your dome, it can bring you to some quick mental conclusions about where you're living and the people living around you.

Conclusion #1: These mu'fuckas is crazy.

Conclusion #2: These mu'fuckas is crazy.

**Conclusion #3: These mu'fuckas right here, boss? . . .
Oh yeah, they crazy.**

That was my first experience with how wild and violent my new community could be. It was my welcome to Liberty City, Miami. I was so far away from Falmouth, Jamaica, that it could have been another planet. I was on new soil—a new soil from which a new Ky-Mani would be forced to grow.

There were always gunshots ringing in the air. Always. You couldn't escape it. And at that time, it never grew in my mind to become a big deal, probably because it didn't seem to be such a big deal to the people of the area. They just didn't care. It was just life. Everybody went on about his or her own daily business like nothing happened. A shooting here. A stabbing there. A body laying dead somewhere. It didn't matter. For those who live in places like this, you know how it is. Our murders don't make the news. Shit pop off, and you mind your business. If it doesn't directly involve you, you mind your business. Still gotta keep living. Still gotta keep surviving. And if you wanna survive this shit, it's usually best to do just that . . . MIND YOUR BUSI-NESS. This means:

Translation #1: When the police come asking questions, *walk the other way and shut the fuck up.*

Translation #2: When you see somebody doing something that they don't want seen, *act like you ain't seen shit and shut the fuck up.*

Translation #3: If you got beef, *call up your people and strap the fuck up.*

These are the Three Secrets of Success when it comes to surviving the streets of Liberty City, Miami.

And so it was.

I was there now. On the ground. So, when in Rome . . . well, you know the rest. I adapted to that mentality and learned to keep it moving, just like everyone else did. *Keep it moving*, partner. No questions. No answers. No snitching. Blind, deaf, and dumb will keep you alive here. This was it. This was my new life in Miami . . . my new atmosphere, my new home. So naturally, after a while, a fish can only reflect the water it's been swimming in. I was about to go from a nice little *Nemo* to a full-scale *Shark* in no time.

It might have all started with my Uncle B, who at that time was hustling herb out of the house. Weed, ganja, sticky-icky, kush, kaya, mary j, cannabis, chronic, hemp, hash . . . whatever you want to call it. He was serving it up to the locals so that we could get caked up a lil' bit to make the ends meet. So day in and day out, while watching cartoons and doing whatever it is that little kids do, at the same time I'm watching mad action going on around my house. There was hella foot traffic, 'cause you know we don't mess with nothing but that good shit from Jamaica, so fools is lining up. Know what I mean?

So, I'm sitting around watching *The Flintstones* or some shit while soaking up the dope game at the same time. It's crazy. Every day I'm watching people coming to the gate of my house asking for my Uncle B. "Hey yo, B here?" "Hey yo B, lemme get that!" Then like clockwork, I'd see Uncle B walk out and give the perp a little baggie of greenery. They would come asking for a little nickel bag or a dime bag or whatever. And Uncle B would go out and serve his customer like it was nothing. And to us, it was exactly that . . . nothing at all.

You have to understand, we Jamaicans. Marijuana to us was like . . . let me see . . . like aspirin is to Americans. It's just something that is and always has been. In Jamaica, it's not legal, but it might as well be, because you see it everywhere, every day, and it's no problem. You're used to that. Police don't front you about it there like they do here. We knew that Jamaican cops arrested you for herb at times, but they were liberal about it. It wasn't that serious. It was somethin' they would really bug you about, because it seemed like it was a thing that almost the entire population did here and there. Okay, maybe a little more than here and there, but it just didn't have the same taint, the same stigma culturally like it does here in the States. To us, a lil' herb is no big deal. So, my Uncle B would serve casually in front of the kids and anyone else. It was almost as innocent as if my grandmother had been selling slices of rum cake out of the back door. That's how innocuous this shit was . . . to us.

On any given day my little cousin and I would be in the yard playing and somebody would stroll through the gate and run it like, "Yo, B here?" We'd just point and the person would head to the door. It was a regular daily thing. Just another day. The people would walk through the gate, holla at Uncle B, pay their money, get their herb, and go on about their business. Well, pretty soon there were a lot more customers coming through that gate, and when people would come and ask for Uncle B, we already knew what they were there for.

So after a while, I just started getting up and getting it myself. That's right. I would get up, go get the weed, and serve it up. At eight and nine years old. *That's bananas!* This makes me laugh now because it's absolutely crazy. We were kids! I've got kids of my own now, and I can't imagine any of them doing some craziness like this. But I need you to remember something. As a kid, I'd seen Uncle B do this day in and day out, and I didn't understand the consequences of this; in Jamaica, you see people sellin' weed, smokin' weed, walkin' through the streets puffin' the herb, and not really worryin' about the cops. We came from an island where it's referred to as *herb. Herb*, not *drugs*. So my mom wasn't sayin' nothin'. My uncle ain't sayin' nothin'. I'm just a kid serving some *herb!* Like a pro. No biggie. You know it's amazing what kids pay attention to and soak in when you think they aren't paying attention in the least.

Naturally things progressed. Before I knew it, when Uncle B wasn't around, the customers acted like they didn't care. And they didn't. They were just there for one thing: *weed*.

And eventually the customers didn't even bother asking for B anymore; they just started coming directly to *me*, and I dealt with it. At this time in my life, it was nothing for a grown man to be standing in front of me asking for a bag of weed. He could have been asking for cupcakes or Twinkies; it would have been the same thing for me. So, now I'm not even ten years old yet and asking a grown man what he wants: nickel or dime? Little bag, nickel. Big bag, dime. It wasn't rocket science. After the man stated his preference, I'd just go get it from the jar, give it to him in one hand, and hold out my other hand to collect. And he would pay me. I'd take the money, and I would put it up somewhere until my Uncle B came home. Done.

I sold my first baggie when I was about eight or nine. And I don't even think my moms knew at that point because we were still getting settled here; she didn't know the difference in the consequences here versus how it is in Jamaica. It was nothing for us. So after a while, it all just became second nature to me. It was just what it was. So, I ended up doing this right up through school. All easy. No problems. If we needed money to eat and couldn't make it anywhere else, we made it on the block. Period. We most definitely weren't going to starve. Nada. Not an option. I'm not really even thinking about the fact that I could go to jail or juvenile detention for this.

Three years later and I'm twelve years old and have been doing this for years without any problems. I was selling product out of the house like it was candy. I had become official. I was part of the program. Of course, I think I'm a man now. But I was also about to get my first taste of how dangerous this was, because up to this point, I didn't take it too seriously. Not yet. Not until what was about to happen happened. That's when I found out how serious this herb was.

One day my Uncle B was on his way out of the house, going somewhere on a run that must have been extremely important. I assumed it was important because before he grabbed his things and mashed out, he came directly over to me and explicitly said, with no question in his eyes, "Listen. No weed. No weed ain't sellin' out the house today. Got it?"

"Yeah," I told him.

Now this is the day when I found out how serious this herb was on the streets of America. Fools is extra hungry out here. Extra. I was a young kid, still not knowing the price of this. But that cherry was about to get popped.

So listen, when all the adults left this time, my Uncle had put a whole suitcase full of herb under the bed. Bricks, you hearin' me? A suitcase full. Think that over. Not a nickel, not a dime, not ten bags, not twenty—a suitcase.

We're still living in a two-bedroom, raggedy little board-house with a big-ass hole in the kitchen. Remember? To me, it's like ten times worse than that shack back in Jamaica. If you're standing at the back door and fall down, ya hit your head on the front door. The space is small. And all this weed is now under the bed. And we're in Liberty City, Miami. The real deal ground zero hood. The fuckin' weed is right under where me and my moms sleep. I don't know what the street value was back then, but I know it was a lot. I remember Uncle B left shortly after he told me what he told me, and there was only me and my little cousin David left. We were the only two people left at home! I'm talking a twelve-year-old and a seven- or eight-year-old. Kids! We might as well have been wearing necklaces made from raw pork chops in a kennel of slobberin' hungry rotweilers. Do you know where we're at?!

So my little cousin David was playing, I think, and I was watching TV. We were doing whatever it is that children do at that age. It was all cool. We had it handled. No worries. No complications. *What could go wrong?* We were just two kids (home alone), chilling with a suitcase full of Jamaica's finest in the other room. Little did we know at the time, we were like sheep waiting for the wolves to show up. And sure enough . . .

All of a sudden I see two people outside the window. I hear the back gate squeak open as one of them comes into the yard. And now I see the other one making a left and heading around to the front door. Okay. Fine. Customers. They're entering the yard in an odd way, but I got it handled.

So I watch the two people walk into the yard from two different directions. Interesting. But no problem. It's just some people coming to ask for weed. Been there, done that, right? Honestly in the moment, this is all kind of strange to me, even as a kid, but in my head, it's still not registering. The whole picture hadn't come together yet. I might have been helping to hustle weed out the door for the last three years like I was a seasoned pro, but I'm still just twelve years old. I'm not yet that quick at this point. But I am quickly developing . . . oh please believe.

Before I know it, one dude is at the front door knocking. *Bam, bam, bam.* So, I'm cool. All I gotta do is restate what Uncle B told me. *No weed today.* I open the door. I see his face. I didn't know him. I looked up at him, and it just was what it was, you know? No problems. He spoke his business.

"Where the weed at?" he asked me.

Okay, fine. Just like I thought. A customer. So I said, "Ain't no weed here."

"Yeah?"

"Nah, no weed," I said.

He didn't seem to be moved by that. He's still standin' there. He's not going on about his business like all the rest. And now his partner is present. He fixed his face squarely, and then he said to me again, "Where the weed at?"

So, I answered back, saying again, "There's no weed here."

Now, in my head, I'm hearing my uncle tell me, "No weed is sellin' out the house today, so there's no weed here." That's my story, and I'm sticking to it. Plus, I'm still stuck on the thought that they're coming to *buy* weed. But this idea is quickly eroding in my mind, especially now that they are all the way *in* my house, acting like they couldn't understand the English I was saying through my Jamaican accent. What is it about "There's no weed here" that they aren't getting?

It wasn't until I overheard one of them say something to the other one that I first started to figure it out. The man kept arguing with the other dude, going back and forth. Then finally I heard one of them say, "Yuh nuh si seh dem a little youth?" He was saying, "Yo, you don't see that? They're kids!" He was trying to make a point about something that didn't sound so good, and that's when I realize that something is really, really not right here. So the next time he asked me, I was ready with some quick thinking. The house is so small that he is standing practically right in front of the weed! That stash is just under the bed! In this little-bitty, tiny-ass house, he was literally perched about two steps from the fuckin' suitcase. He could drop a quarter right now and it would roll and hit the side of the mu'fucking suitcase of bricks and please believe . . . we're dead. So, quick thinking. I remembered where we used to keep the baggies in a plastic kind of cookie jar thing. I was mapping out where that was so that by the next time he asked meagain, and he did, I said, "Alright. I'll give you the weed."

I walked over to the cupboard and I got down the cookie jar. He grabbed the cookie jar and opened it, looking for the mother lode. It had only a little bit of weed in there, a bag, and about forty dollars. I don't know how much weed it was, but it definitely wasn't a suitcase full. The jar was basically empty.

He looked at me and said in island dialect, "All of it this?"
I said, "All of it dat."

They studied me. They studied each other. And then the both of them walked out of the house.

My people. Hold on. Breathe, right? That shit was crazy. I was a little-ass kid. What was I gonna do? I had a little weight on me, but I was still a featherweight contender compared with a grown man. And two of 'em? My cousin and I would have been done. Both of us. RIP . . . you know what I mean?

But I remember this as clearly as what I did this morning. The whole time this is happening, I'm not nervous or anything at all like that. I'm just calm, collected, and coolheaded about it. That day I found out something about myself. I found something that I continued to see and use. I found that when the pressure is on and when I'm realizing that something is wrong, that's how I naturally respond. No panic. It's just quick thinking that kicks in to resolve the situation. When you're in that hood type of environment for a while, whether you're aware of it or not, whether you use it or not, it just starts to become a part of you, and you learn these things. Through the ether, I guess. You pick up on it. You have to. Everybody has to. Just to survive. The little kid. The adult. Men. Women. Criminals. Cops. Roaches, rats, or whatever. You're in the midst of predators—somebody's always trying to get at somebody and one day that somebody might be you. You are in a hostile environment of poor people who are naturally and occasionally pissed off or hostile about that. Heads are hungry out here, and you get to lookin' like a *meal* to them. And like I told you before, I'm not the one lookin' to get eaten. So, for me, if you look like you're even just *thinking* about licking your chops . . . I'm gonna move on you before you move on me. Period. It's about survival. And on that day, in that very moment, I really got how this type of quick thinking can SAVE . . . YOUR . . . LIFE.

Uncle B was the first adult to return later that day. I had bad news to report, and I knew I had to man up and give him the full rerun on it. I remember stepping to Uncle B and telling him in dialect, "Some people come for rob the house today."

You can probably guess the look he had on his face; it was clear that he wasn't a happy man about this. I explained to him exactly what happened step by step, in complete detail. I told him exactly what they ended up taking, which was the weed that was stuffed in the jar, but that was it. He looked under the bed, popped the suitcase open, and checked the whole load. It was all there.

At this time, my moms was working a gig at this Office Depot type place. She was just getting home from work when my uncle had to sit her down to talk. He dropped the day's events on her. She wasn't at all happy either. Of course, my moms immediately comes straight in to me and starts interrogating me about what happened and making sure I was okay. I just sat down and spilled my guts to her, giving her the play-by-play details like I did for Uncle B, and she listened. I told her about these men coming through the gate from the back, then at the front door, and then into the house drilling me with, "Where the weed at? Where the weed at?"

Oh. She. Was. Pissed. Pissed. Pissed. *Piiiiiissed.*

My mom kept a little strap on her—a lil' old-school burner. She had a .38 snub-nosed revolver. Anita ain't for any bullshit. When it comes to madness like this, threatening her child—no, not gonna happen. Hear me . . . not gonna happen. That's who my mother is.

She left and went out for a little bit, saying she was going to try to find out who the hell came into our house. While she was gone, I had a little time to think about everything. It was all coming to me in a different light now that I'd seen how my mother and uncle reacted to it. My mom definitely didn't plan on us *ever* gettin' caught slipping like that again. She was serious about that.

I remember when she finally came back into the house. It was evening by then. Early evening it was, to be exact. I think about seven o'clock or so. I can remember it was just getting dark outside, and she immediately comes and gets me and takes me out into the backyard. I didn't know what was happening. I'm standing there. I'm looking at her. And then she straight pulls her .38 out, and says, "Give me your hand."

Your mother tells you to do something, ya do it, right? I put out my hand. She looks at me, and I look back at her.

My hand is still out. And then she puts the gun right in it. *Whoa.* This was serious business, for real.

"Raise it above your head," she instructed.

Your mother tells you to raise a gun above your head, ya do it, right? I did.

"Pull the trigger one time."

Whoa, whoa. Hold on. Okay, so look. As you can imagine, life is coming at me really fast. I'm twelve years old, co-dealing herb since I was nine, just got fronted by two grown men trying to rob us for weed (probably some neighborhood killers), and now my mother has just put a loaded .38 in my hand and is telling me to squeeze off a round into the air. *My dude, whaaaaaaat?* Shouldn't I be somewhere playing a video game or something like that? Maybe in some other life. I lived on 22nd and 90 Street in Liberty City. Not a lot of heads for games over there. And my mother definitely wasn't about games on this night. This is the first time I have held a gun—let alone, a loaded gun. Cherry. Very. Popped.

"Raise it above your head and pull the trigger one time," she said again.

I'm holding the gun. It's a little heavy in my hands, but I got it. I'm not as cool, calm, and collected now, but I'm there. I'm in the moment. I asked her, "Is it gonna kick?"

Thinking back, I don't know how I knew to ask this. I'm guessing it was all from watching TV.

She then said to me, "Yeah, it's gon' kick. Just hold it firm and squeeze."

Okay. I got the gun. I'm gripping it tight. My arms are cocked out over my head in a pyramid, and I'm holding this thing in the air. I said to her, "But what if when it kick, it fall out my hand?"

She said, "Nah, you hold it firm and squeeze. It's not gonna fall out your hand."

I'm stuck now. She looks over at me and I guess she's starting to tell I was nervous about it. So she takes the gun out of my hands. I watch her. She makes sure that I see her. She holds it straight up over her own head and squeezes out two hot ones right there on the spot. *Blauh! blauh!* That shit was loud and too damned close. But she gave me a demonstration I would never forget. This ain't like my mom teaching me how to body rock and shake off opponents in soccer. This is my mom teaching me how to blast somebody if I have to. *Who is this woman?*

Word to Jah. After that, my mom brings me back into the house and replaces the shells, putting two bullets back into the revolving case. I never did shoot the gun that night. But she took the reloaded strap and put the hot gun under my pillow.

She then sits me down and looks me in the eye, "I'm going out on the road for a little bit. If anything come into this house, any face that you don't recognize, you take this gun and you aim and you pull that trigger. When I get home, I'll deal with the rest."

That moment was a changing moment in my life.

My mother just put a gun in my hand. Can you imagine the feeling of your mother placing a gun in your hand and saying to you what she said to me? I mean this is not a case where you're with your boys and you just snuck the gun out pretending, showing off or something stupid. This is your mother, the bona fide person who raised you, and she just gave you orders to shoot any damned thing that comes into the house that you don't recognize. Those are soldier's orders.

So when I look back and I reflect on that story, I know at that point—right then and there—a lot of things changed for me. That's where I really got the understanding and perspective of the severity of what just happened or what could have just happened to me. That changed a lot in me. Cherry very, very popped. As far as I'm concerned, that was my first step toward manhood. I was protector of the premises.

Life goes on. And life went on. After that point, everything kind of fell back into place, back into the same routine. Nothing changed. I'm still selling weed out of the house as a young lad. I'm growing. I'm going to school. We're not really focused on or even contemplating the possible consequences. We're just focused on surviving. We're also focused on staying clear of the law, knowing not to trust the police no time, no place, nowhere. In my neighborhood, we already knew that when you saw those boys coming, it was time to just lay low.

We even got hip to their routine. Tuesdays and Thursdays they would ride the block heavy, and we knew to just chill out on those days. Simple. I was raised in this. Raised in the inner city . . . with nothing. Liberty City, Miami, Dade County. And when it goes down for you like this, you gotta know how to turn your nothing into something and keep going, keep moving. And that's what we did. Judge if you want to. And many will. But if I had been in your high-class shoes, I would've probably been walking the same walk you walked. But since I wasn't, I was walking my own walk in the shoes I was given.

The struggle continued; therefore, the hustle continued. Things definitely got hard around this time. Definitely. 'Cause at this point, just to be raw and real, we still aren't getting any money from the estate. Reaganomics was in full effect. I mean it was a *fight*. No money was coming in. My mom was working a nine to five, and it was still a struggle. Around this same time, when we did finally get a chance to gain some independence and move out of my grandma's house, it was just across the street. We broke free—a little bit. It was overpopulated in my grandma's house, just like it was back in Jamaica. So, we moved to a little place where we were just basically renting a room. It was a three-bedroom house, with each being rentable. Only one room was completely ours, and it had a bathroom attached. It was one of those setups where everybody shares a kitchen, but at least it still was a place of our own. Now we had *our* little place of the world.

Moving was cool, even though the move was just across the way. It gave everybody some more space. At my grandma's, they needed to bring down the head count for a while, and it was good to have some room just to ourselves for a change. For the most part, things were very different but exactly the same, if that makes any sense. It's still Liberty City. It's still drama. It's still a struggle to maintain. I'm still living in a neighborhood where gangstas, dealers, and crackheads freely roam the street, having their way. There's still this crackhead living right outside our building—and to this day, he's a mainstay on the block. We still sit and talk occasionally whenever I visit the Ave. He's always got something of value to say, if I'm listening. Oddly enough, I just saw him last week. But back then, I was still a kid with all this raw shit in front of me. As a matter of fact, the crackhead used to show me the crack rocks, smokin' it in front of me and then schoolin' me on it, saying, "Listen, you make sure you stay away from this shit. See how it fucked me up?"

This is what he's telling me. He was telling me as a young one, you don't want to start. So I'd ask him, "Well, why don't you stop, if you see what it's doing to you?"

He'd say, "Man, when this shit gets ahold of you, that's it. It have you."

And all the same, while he was telling me this, he was flaming his pipe, smokin' this rock right in front of me. When he did, I would back off. I didn't want *that* shit. I didn't know how dangerous *that* shit was. I didn't want to smell *that* shit.

I didn't want to be around *that* shit. No how. No way.

Every day that I went outside, just seeing his condition was like a constant TV public service announcement telling me, "Don't fuck with this crack shit." I didn't want to touch it. I was convinced . . . for now at least. It's all kind of unbelievable to me today. I just remember, being exposed to all of this as a very young boy, and it's incredible to think about that now.

Things were about to really ramp up. My mom and I were about to kick into a new gear of survival mode. We were doing everything we could to not have to turn back around. It was at this new home for my mom and I that she started her own hustling. Her hustle was separate from Uncle B's . Times were like that. It is crazy to think back on this now.

My mom had some very good friends, a lot of them just happened to be the gangsta type. You know, they do what they do. She had some of these friends who were friends from Jamaica, old friends from school she knew growing up, and others from old neighborhoods she'd lived in. In the neighborhood itself were many of my Jamaican people, maybe five or six Jamaican homes in the two-block radius. So all of this was fortunate for me because I was able to sustain some of my customs and culture. And my mother was able to get plugged in to the game.

I remember one day at the house when my mom came to me and said, "One of my friends wants me to do something for him."

I'm still very young at this point, so naturally I asked, "Okay, what is it?"

I could ask her questions like this with no problem or disrespect to her authority. That's one thing I appreciate about my mom. We could get down like that. She was big on us being a team, a family, a unit. My age didn't matter. We were in this together. She didn't do anything without me first knowing. She would always let me in on exactly what was going down. Just because I was a child, she didn't assume I was too weak to handle things. She respected my intelligence and judgment, and for the most part, she treated me that way. And she was about to drop a big one on me.

She told me flat out, "My friend wants me to move a snowpack from Miami to Pittsburgh."

It's amazing that I still remember all these details, but its not every day that your mom is talking about moving some weight, so you tend to remember shit like this.

"What do you think about this, Ky-Mani?" she asked.

I said to her, "Well, how are you gonna do it?"

Now listen. This is some more left-of-center shit. This is a mother-son conversation when I'm twelve or thirteen years old.

She told me, "I'm gonna carry one pack on each hip."

"What if when you're going through the metal detector then, you beep?" I asked?

She thought about this and said to me, "Nah. I'm not gon' beep going through the metal detector 'cause I'm not gonna wear no jewelry. The pants I'm gonna wear has a drawstring and I'll wear a baggy shirt. A linen shirt with linen pants, all loose so there is no metal at all."

I thought about it and envisioned it as meticulously and as clearly as I could. "Alright, cool," I said.

That's how I remember that night.

She was supposed to leave early in the evening on the next day, so she took me across the street to my grandma's house, where I had to stay because she would be gone for the weekend.

The night before she left, she came to see me and told me, "Alright. I'm gonna go to the airport now."

So I said, "Okay. You have that stuff?"

Sure enough, she had it. She showed it to me. She had it on each hip. I looked at it. I said, "Cool. Okay." In my mind, I guess she was ready for business.

I said "okay," but at the time I realize I was so free with that part of it is because I didn't think that snowflakes had an odor. I was at ease about it all. She left. I had to fall back at my grandma's house for the weekend. It was all in motion. I spent the weekend doing what I do, but my mind was consumed with my mom and what was happening with her. Like anybody, I didn't want anything to happen to my mother. I kept wondering, *What was going to happen to her?*

Days later, I finally got word back. The mystery was finally over. I finally found out what happened. She came back! She got through. She got to Pittsburgh and back with no problems. What she did come back with was three grand in her pocket, which is some monkey money for the risk she's taking, but for us at that time, it was a big damned deal. Three thousand dollars. That was *dough*. We had never seen that much money at one time. At that point I don't even think we had ever seen one grand at one time. And now . . . three? For us, it was very big frickin' deal. Believe that.

Those were good days for us. I remember my mom taking me shopping for clothes and everything like that. We were trying to tie up some loose ends that had been loose for a while. But don't get me wrong about Anita; she always kept me clean. My clothes were clean no matter what our situation was . . . no matter what we were dealing with. My clothes were always ironed, and my shirt and shoes were always clean. This is just who she was, regardless of money. She was an impeccable mother in this way. But with this three grand in hand, it was like we had entered a different world. She took me to the mall; she took me to the movies to see whatever the hot flick was at the time. We just had a great time together. We breathed a little bit. And it felt good.

Yep, we were on some *Cosby Show* shit for a minute, living the good life with that three grand. Spirits were running high, naturally. But if you don't keep the hustle up, eventually the money is gonna run low again.

Awhile later my mother comes to me again. She sits me down and says, "They want me to make that trip again."

I begin thinking about that three grand again—the movies, the mall, the clothes. I look at her and I say, "Alright, cool."

She makes that run up north and she returns to Miami. She shows me the dough again. No problems. This is starting to look good. And this officially becomes the new hustle. She starts making this run on the regular. We're eating.

Life was good. This hustle was taking the edge off of things. But you know how it goes. Like all good things, they eventually get knocked off track a bit. And this money train was about to run straight off the tracks and into some complications.

I remember one time my mom came to me to tell me that they now wanted her to take some marijuana up north. She said to me, "They want me to go again, and this time they want me to bring some weed."

Whoa.

I looked at her. "Weed?" I said.

In my mind, this wasn't sitting too peacefully. In my mind, I knew that weed had an odor. And I knew about the dogs and the whole sniffing routine. I immediately told her, "Nah, you can't go through the airport with no weed. Nah." I wasn't feeling it. I said, "What about the dogs?"

She started telling about the process of how they were going to pack it so that the dogs wouldn't be able to smell it. And after she went on about what they told her, I said, "I don't trust that."

She looked at me, straight into my eyes. "You wanna come?" she asked. No joke.

Wait a minute. *Do I want to come? What is she talking about?*

Then she clarified, "Do you want to come to where they pack it?"

I'm stunned by this, of course.

She went on, "You wanna come see how they're doing it?"

No joke. So, of course, I said, "Yeah."

And that was that. It was done. It was decided. I guess she figured if it could possibly impact my life too, she wanted me to have full disclosure; she wanted me to know the lengths that she would go through to make sure that we survive. She was going to take me to see the process. I was going. Done.

My mother didn't waste any time. Before I know it, it's like I'm in a movie. My mom and I roll out of the house. We're going to see how it all gets done. It's like some Bonnie and Clyde bizness—mother and son version. Riders.

I'm laughing about this now, but back then, this was serious business. My mother and I have an unbreakable bond, but I realize that we have bonded over some real nontraditional shit. But the point is, we were bonding. And we are bonded like glue to this day. Not a lot of people can say that. I'm blessed in that way. I love my mom. And she'd never have to speak a word to tell me that she loves me, because the history we have together tells me that, every day. There is no mystery. There are no cracks for doubt. There is lived evidence. And for this, it makes those three words, when she says them, mean so much more than when others say them.

So there we were. I'm still a young boy. I'm riding with my mother, and we roll up on this house. We go in, and as real as these pages in your hands, as a juvenile, I'm standing over grown men as they pack the weed like professionals. They're operating like scientists. They're putting fabric softener here, then encasing wraps around this, then squirting oily shit around that and this other. I didn't know what the hell they were doing, but they were working. I just watch and observe. Inspecting. I paid total and full attention until they were completely finished. After all, this was my mother and I wasn't trying to lose her too. So this was a serious thing for me. This was a serious consideration.

When the packing process was over and I had seen every segment of it, my mother took me outside and questioned me about it.

"So, what you think?" she asked.

I looked at her again. Without hesitation, I said flat out, "No. I don't trust it."

Period. And that was that. No more questions. No, "Why?" No, "Well, what if I . . ." No, "Well, you're a little kid, so . . ." None of that. I flat out said, "No. I don't trust it." She asked. I gave her my answer. She heard. And that was that. She didn't go. End of story.

My mother immediately told her people that it wasn't going to happen and that she wasn't the one to make this run. They had to find somebody else. And they did. Finding someone was never a problem. There are plenty of hungry people out there ready to put it all on the line. They soon found another one willing, and the new girl made the run.

Something clicked in my mind right then and there. By making this decision and having my mother abide by it, I was getting a sense of my own power, and a sense of her trust in me. Something was telling me that it was time for me to put it all on the line for myself, for my mother, and for our survival. She was doing it. She was putting herself at risk for me. It was clearly time for me to step up and become the man of the house. If it was survival by all means necessary, then that was the game I was ready to play. That was my attitude about it. If push kept coming to shove, I would do what I had to do. If it meant I had to sell all the drugs in America, then that's exactly what I was going to do.

Fifth Lesson Learned:

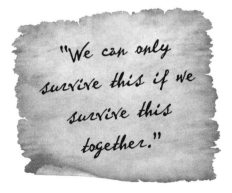

"We can only survive this if we survive this together."

6

Crack Got No Clock
(Unnecessary Badness 2)

I WAS RAISED ON A CORNER WITH ABOUT THIRTEEN KIDS—most without fathers; all very, very rowdy; and all ready to go at it for whatever, at any given time.

I now have a fifteen-year-old son. At times I yell at him or rough him up a little bit—in a fatherly way, nothing abusive. I have laid hands on him a few times to spank or discipline him. But when I sit down and I reflect, I think, *Wow. He's fifteen.* When I was fifteen, I was out of control. Compared with what I was doing at his age, he's a *saint.* At age fifteen, I was strapped day and night. And every night, when my grandmother would go to bed and when I was supposed to be sleep, I would get up and go right back out on the corner and serve crack. Fifteen. A spanking wasn't gonna do it for me.

In my neighborhood, I had a lot of friends—most of whose fathers were dead. You know about mine, but most of theirs were dead from gunshot wounds. *That's* the kind of neighborhood I'm in. I'm in that kind of surrounding. And I'm around a bunch of kids who long ago stopped giving a fuck. So naturally you start to be exposed to everything you can imagine that you're not supposed to be exposed to. After seven years, coming up together as rowdy-ass kids, my whole set, we got our hands on guns. What's a soldier without the tools for war?

Let me paint the picture for you. It's Miami. We're in the ghetto. The temperature is bubbling. The mood is violent. At that time, my block is the hot block in the area. Everybody hangs out on my block. Everybody. There's a resident crackhead who lives across the street in the bushes, and he's got all kinds of fuckin' traps set up, 'cause he's ex-military coming from Vietnam, where he learned all this shit. He set up all kinds of booby traps for the police. I remember walkin' through that bush one time and just hearin' some dude screamin', "Oh no! Oh no!" This crackhead dude had dug a four-foot to five-foot hole with sharpened pegs and shit sticking up from the bottom; then he covered it with leaves. He was outta his mind. He said, "That's for when them pigs be running through here, to fuck 'em up." Then he'd start laughing. I'm guessing he was tired of being harassed by local police. God forbid some little children were playing around there. But this is the tone of my neighborhood.

My neighborhood is virtually all juveniles. Although there were some adults in the neighborhood slangin' and doin' what they're doin', it's really us, the juveniles, who had control of the neighborhood. A lot of these adults didn't really realize how dangerous we kids were. They really didn't know what was going on below the surface. There were ten-, eleven-, twelve-, thirteen-, and fourteen-year-olds roaming the streets, and all of them were strapped, but nobody knew. For us it was no different than when nations proliferate. I mean, seriously, what's the difference? If Israel gets strapped up on the nuclear tip, then Iran is going to try to do the same thing. Naturally. And if you have some beef with some heads across the street and they're rolling with some heavy metals, then what do you have to do? You gotta even the playing field and balance the tension out. Get guns.

That's how it was. You want what your enemy has just in case it all goes down. This was the environment. So many want to point the finger in disgust at what they consider hood rats and all the drama that goes down in the trap when their tax dollars are doing the same thing on the national level. That's funny to me. What's the difference between two nations beefin' with armies versus sets of kids beefin' in the streets with guns? Nothing but the reasons they're using to do it.

So naturally after a while, that scenario became us. You know, we got our own ideas about how we were going to survive these streets. Let me tell you, a couple of my friends had beef with some kids who lived across the street. At this time, we were in elementary and middle school, growing up together since third grade, so you can understand how young we are. I mean, we are *young*. Again when I think about my child now being the age I was back then, my child is a saint.

And hold on, let me tell you, at that age, in that hood, the simple task of just walking to the corner store was intense, especially because I was raised in a neighborhood where these kids weren't afraid to shoot. They just *weren't*. Period. It wasn't an issue for them. I don't even think they had any concept of what they were really, *really* doing and how long the consequences were. I mean, at that point, when your own life is so compromised, the life or death of another has no real meaning. How can it mean something if you have no real meaning in your own life? There was no fear of death. Hell, if they could articulate their feelings, they were probably thinking death might even be better. So who cared? *Nobody.*

Naturally, with this type of mentality, anything was possible. I mean, whatever it is to do, they were willing and ready to do it. In broad daylight or at midnight—it made no difference whatsoever. I had a set of friends among whom this was the common mentality—the group mentality. If it came down to it, you'd just do it. And we'd all do it together.

So that's life right now and we're living it. Juveniles, roaming the block, hard. And naturally, being in a neighborhood where we're exposed to crack, dope pushers, and whatnot, please believe we're gonna get ideas. Believe that. We were getting ideas of our own about how we were most definitely going to find a way to scrape a little of that shit off here for ourselves. No one else is gonna eat and feast while our lil' hungry asses just sit back and watch. We're just gonna watch and not get some too? Uh-uh, not happening. Somebody was gonna get got, so that we could get too. Period.

I remember my uncle used to have these suitcases like the one he left in the house when I was twelve. And when he did have them, we used to go in there and hit it up a little. We could do this because Uncle B didn't seem to be checking, so we used to just go in there and pinch him off and bag that shit it up ourselves. After that we would just squad up and start hustlin' the block with this weed and start puttin' money away on the side. Hustle peeped. Hustle learned. Hustle done. We did this until it was time to move up. The whole time we were the boys who had *the weed* around there, and that was cool, but everybody knew in the back of their minds that it was *crack* that sold.

So we did that. We played our position on the block. We started our little weed selling operation—me and the boys together—on the side. But at the same time, I'm still sellin' weed at the house for my man Kirk, another Jamaican who lived just down the street from me. He's sellin' weed out of his house for his mom. On the next block is my boy Courtney, and he's sellin' weed over there for his uncle. We're out here doin' it anyway for everybody else, so we start talking about doing it for ourselves. And, of course, that day came. It was time to try to step it up to the next level. And to us, the next level was stackin' enough paper to be able to go buy the coke, cook the fuckin' crack, and then sell it. Next level. It's just the way of the neighborhood. We were about to graduate, and the school was the streets.

At this same time, we were having some beef around the neighborhood. They had just shot one of my homeboys and that same friend of mine, Kirk, who I was selling weed and getting this money with, they bucked him up on the block. You know how fools do. Around this time he's now probably about fifteen. He's walking home one day . . . but he's walking home with a gun in a brown paper bag. Ready. So eventually the drama kicks in. This cat and his little brother pull up on Kirk right on the avenue just a little bit before his house. They made their little threats, made their little remarks. Back and forth it went. Words were had. So the dudes roll down the street and make a U-turn. They came back and pulled up on Kirk. And with no question, Kirk points his gun right into the car and shoots. Luckily the kid didn't die; he took the two shots to the chest and lived. But from that time, the beef was on.

All of this was in 1992, right after Hurricane Andrew had ripped through Miami. It was a Category 5 hurricane that just tore down the South Florida homesteads like they were made from paper. It was the same hurricane that had just leveled the Caribbean. And everything around our whole area right there was done. It was devastated.

Because of the hurricane and the destruction at that time, curfews were in effect, but at the same time, the tensions on the block were extra hot. The cops weren't really trying to patrol in the hood to really enforce some frickin' curfews. They wanted go home to their wife and kids. When they drove down the street chirping, the kids might stop momentarily, but it wasn't like the police were really holdin' it. It wasn't in their interest. What property was it around there for them to protect? These were poor folks.

So we're still in this situation. And for me, it was probably one of my lowest moments, although I wasn't really even thinking about it at the time. So you know my set, my riders, we were goin' through this beef and now we have some guns—but not the right ones, you know? We were holdin' a .380, a little .22, and an old rusty .38, you know. The dudes who were across the street were comin' from real dope money, so as far as we know, they have big fire. We seein' they have the Cadillacs over there and the whole setup. G'd up. Okay. Not a problem.

Obviously, my next thought was like anyone's. I'm thinking that we need some real guns to handle this. Proliferation, right? It was time to come up with a master plan. I already knew that an uncle on my father's side had just bought a whole cache of guns—AK's, M-16's, 9 mm's, and a .40. He had a whole collection. But I'm the one who's living in a war zone. When I went to my other grandma's house, my dad's mom, everything was so nice and peaceful. And all the damned houses were big, with manicured lawns—and you didn't see any neighbors. You just saw little white kids riding down the street in their go-karts and all the things that life was supposed to be—or at least what I thought it was gonna be for me. So, I remember going through that beef and sayin', "What we need is some fuckin' guns right now. And I know where some guns at." Master plan was in action.

During all the drama of the hurricane disaster, when that whole thing was hitting the city, I rolled out to my other grandma's house. No one was there, and I saw this as a grand opportunity. Either I was going to do this or not. Either we were gonna get overpowered with gunfire and die like soldiers or we were gonna have the means to fight back and ride like soldiers.

Sitting outside that house, that beautiful house in that beautiful neighborhood—and it was still beautiful to me, hurricane or not—I finally made up my mind. In that moment, I said to myself, *Know what? I'mma take these guns right here.* And I went inside very much uninvited. I didn't want anything else but the guns. That was my focus. And the whole time I'm bagging them up, I'm thinking, *We got guns now. We 'bout to go shoot this shit up. Period. Them boys 'cross the way got a bad one coming. It's about to be a real problem.*

So I took the guns and rolled back to the city. As soon as I got there, of course, I immediately strapped up all my boys. We got that heavy machinery now. Think it over. We're fifteen and sixteen years old now. I have an AK hidden in the attic of my homeboy's house. I'm walkin' around with a Glock 15 shooter with an infrared beam on it. That was a 10 mm. Not a 9 mm . . . a 10 mm. So I pull up to my boy on the street and give him new a 9 mm to hold. My other boy got a 40. So now? Please believe. We were back on the block fresh. Beams and everything. We were thinking, *Oh yeah. It's gon' be a serious problem out here.*

This is when we were a solid unit. Unshakable. Unbreakable. We were together every day. We walked to school together, we walked home together, we hung out in the neighborhood together, and we made money on the block together, day and night. We were it. Period.

At the time, I kept the two rifles. I handed out the handguns and kept the AK and an M-16.

Then one of the boys, who's passed on now (may God bless his soul), he stepped to me and said, "Yo, my brother wanna know if you'll sell him the M-16."

Whaaat? At first, I told him, "Nah."

"Yo, they really want it. They really need it," he argued.

Okay. He was puttin' on the pressure more and more.

So, at that time, that's when those little mini-motorcycles came out. I was just seein' them for the first time and naturally my boys and I all wanted one. So now I'm on a mission to get one, and that's where my head was at that moment. And now I'm thinkin' the opportunity had just arrived.

I step to my boy who was pressuring me on the M-16. I told him, "Alright. How much money you got? What he wanna do?"

"He don't got no money, but he said he'll give you an ounce of coke."

I replied, "An ounce of coke? We don't need no coke. What about crack?" We're kids, right? And I'm tellin' you, this is a real conversation right here. We don't know yet that *coke* sells on the corner, but we for damn sure know that *crack* sells.

So my man said, "Alright, let's go around there."

This was it. This was our chance to get brand new on the block. It's what we were waiting for. It was our chance to move up. I went to my spot and got the M-16. I just took the frickin' rifle out and put that bitch under a sheet, jumped on the bicycle, and rode it over there like it was nothing. Now keep in mind, this is a fuckin' top-of-the-line M-16 with a high-powered scope on it. This ain't for play. So when we get to his brother's spot, we go in the house and we're having words, workin' it out. That's when he shows me the coke.

"I told him we don't want coke," I said. "We need crack."

"A'ight," he said. "Well, this is it. I'll cook it up for y'all."

"A'ight, cool."

We were sold.

Now, we in there watching him cook that shit up, doing

what he had to do, and he gave it to us in a *cookie*. I gave him the M-16 rifle. Business done. Transaction complete. We took the cookie back, cut it down, and bagged the shit up. When we went to the store to get baggies, they knew what the damned bags was for, but they didn't give a shit how old you were. We could have been eight years old. Whatever you wanted, you got it. That's it. Done. We moved up. We just went from them *weed boys* to them *crack boys*. That was big shit. That was like moving from JV to varsity. We were brand new players on a whole new field.

You gotta understand; the corner was like a "hood pharmacy." You could get whatever you needed to numb the pains of ghetto life. Relief was right on the corner if you wanted it. So we were ready to get out there with the best of the pharmacists and serve. We were ready to hit the block hard. So what we did was develop a system. All the adults were out during the daytime doin' their thing. But at midnight when they turned it in, we stayed out. At midnight . . . that's when we cut it on.

On any given night we'd go in like its time to go to sleep, you know. Bedtime. And at that time my uncle had moved out the house and was livin' in another part of the city. So when he would finally go home, the young boys would come out, because crack don't have no clock. Crackheads just didn't cut off. They were fiendin' twenty-four-seven. So while Uncle B was gone, we're out there doin' our thing and makin' money—a lot of money. Like I said, we moved up.

So now, we had it. We had a system, and it ran like clockwork. When the bigger heads went in, the little heads came out. When the bigger heads were sleeping, the little heads were waking up the block. Game. And there was a lot of money to be made. I don't know if the adults knew how much paper they were leaving on the table, but we knew—'cause we were scraping it. This shit was working. We were stackin'. We were knottin' big chips. I was about to go get a whole bag of rubber bands, you hearin' me? It was fresh on the block, boy. It was all good. Well . . . until my uncle found out about it.

Busted. Yep. After a while, my uncle starts gettin' word about some new product on the avenue. And this is not good. (Or you can say it is good, when you look at the long-term effects, for me at least. I can't say it went the same for everybody else.) But he found out. And it all put a serious pause on my paper run.

The neighborhood talks. It's natural. How it happened was indirectly. We were gettin' good pub on the block, but all good publicity ain't good publicity. Not in our case. It was one of those same crackheads poppin' off at the mouth who led to it all being shut down. He lost out. And we lost out.

The crackhead hit up the corner one day to buy some rocks, but he didn't come on our clock. But like I said, crack don't have no clock. Crack doesn't sleep day or night. Crack burns when it needs to burn. So the crackhead hit the corner to get the rocks he was used to gettin', but we weren't there. And when the crack dealer who was there tried to sell him rocks, the crackhead told him, "Nah, uh-uh. I don't want it from you. I want to see them Jitts. Them Jitts' shit is way fatter than any other shit." They used to call our young asses "Jitterbugs," and we were getting a reputation among the crackheads cause we cut up the cookie into some fat-ass rocks. We were upending the market. And his remark is what got us busted for what we were doing at night. Word went out. We were exposed. Exposed in two ways. We were exposed that we were out here actually in business for ourselves, #1, and what we were out here selling is crack, #2. Fat crack at that.

My uncle got wind of it all and made it clear that he disapproved. Then later I was slippin' and left some rocks in a bomb lying out. My moms found it. And of course this sent her *off the rack*. She went into full panic 'cause she immediately thought I was smokin' crack. I had to calm it all down and explain. "No. Never," I told her. "I was selling it."

This wasn't good news, but it was way better than the first assumption. My mom and uncle strongly let it be known that they thought I was playing out of bounds . . . way out of bounds.

At that point, and at that part of it, I let it go. That crack was something different, and when I saw that my family was really, really, really pissed off, upset, and disappointed about the fact that I even *thought* about taking the route that I was taking, I just let that fade out. Wasn't the hustling all for family anyway? So we could come up? If, in the end, it wasn't gonna be something that they were feeling, would there be a point to this? I'm about my family above all things.

Plus at this time I'm still ahead in the game 'cause my uncle still doesn't know how we came about this whole hustle. Pinchin' off his shit. My uncle still doesn't know that I have a cache of heavy artillery in the house—stashed, locked, loaded, and ready for havoc. He still didn't know about that. All that he knows is that we're selling crack and, in his eyes, that shit ain't nowhere near cool. I didn't get caught by the cops, but I got caught by my family. I was lucky. So I let that part of it go.

Looking back, I've always had this fascination with guns. And I don't know if *fascination* is the word I'm looking for, but it was always something I felt comfortable with. And while growing up, it was most definitely something that I felt was a necessity. The straps were going to stay. The other dudes on the avenue had theirs, so therefore I needed mine. That was the neighborhood. That was the regime under which we lived. That's what took place. And the bigger heads, the dudes and the hustlers on the street, they taught you this. It was an open-air market. And I wanted some market share. I was doin' what I felt I needed to do to come up.

I continued heavily with the sellin' of the herb, of course, but I stopped messin' with that other thing. My boys, many of them, went on and bigged up on it. Not a lot of them are living today. Others are eating up time behind bars. I like the nice things in life, too, like the next man. And I saw how those boys was gettin' it. Crack just don't have no clock. Yeah. It was true. We found out that crack don't have no clock, but maybe it does have a calendar. And eventually that number comes up, that fateful day, and that shit catches up with you one way or another. But that's the ways of the trap . . . the neighborhood.

Life gives you a fucked up hand, and you can't just throw it in. You already here. You go ahead and try the best you can with it. Bluff. Sometimes you lose. Bluff. Sometimes you win.

A Soldier's Roll Call:
(You Are Not Forgotten.)

Kirk
Currently Incarcerated

Courtney aka Bird
Currently Incarcerated

Dwayne
RIP

Jerome
RIP

Screw
Legally Employed with Family

Al
RIP

Wayne
Still Hustlin'

Deek
Just Released; Legally Employed

Nose
Still Hustlin'

Skinny Man
Incarcerated—Life Sentence

Ervin
Featured Twice on First 48 Hours on A&E, but back on the Streets

Sixth Lesson Learned:

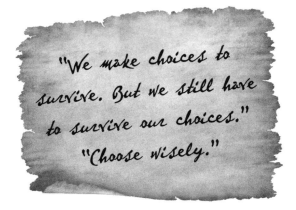

"We make choices to survive. But we still have to survive our choices."
"Choose wisely."

7

Never Back Down
(Unnecessary Badness 3)

IT DOESN'T MATTER IF THE BOYS IS IN THE HOOD WHEN THE HOOD IS IN THE BOY. Listen. When there's not a father in the house, it's easy to find a father on the block. And as boys, my crew and I were taught everything by these dudes on the Ave. Everything. We got schooled by the hustlers and the dealers. And what they didn't teach, we just watched and learned for ourselves. On that block, we got it in, for sure.

We were young, but we were far from innocent. We were growing up, fast. But we were still little kids as far as I'm concerned. We were wildin' daily on the block and were into everything we could get into, with our rock bombs somewhere stashed off in the bush. You name it, we were doing it. We were just up to no good. Wildin' out. We were doing our dirt, and we thought we were doing it the smart way. We were just doing what we saw the bigger heads on the block do. But we weren't thinking about the consequences. Nobody thought like that. All we thought was there's no way they could catch us. We never thought about what would happen if they actually did. We felt we were on top of our game and there was no way we were gettin' busted.

I may have eventually backed off the crack hustle, but I was going full steam on everything else. I was headed in a bad direction, in the wrong lane and speedin'. It was obvious that a crash was coming, and coming soon.

My moms started to realize that she would have to get me out of that neighborhood. It was the only chance to save me from me. I think the crack episode scared her. So she did what she had to do to make it happen. We moved farther south to an area called Kendall. Kendall was a south suburb in Miami-Dade County. It was like night and day compared with Liberty City. I can remember when we were in the process of moving and just peeping the whole new area. I thought, *How could all of this be the same city?* We were rolling down the streets, and all I could notice was that the medians were so nice and neatly kept with palm trees in them. It was a whole different world. There were apartments everywhere, and the streets were really clean. This was definitely going to be a new environment. We finally pulled into our destination. Our new home was a complex called *The Townhomes of Kendall.*

Remembering the great disappointment I experienced on my first day after moving to Liberty City, you'd think I'd be happy with a new clean area, nicer housing, and no shots ringing in the air. But by this time I was a different dude. I was a whole different creation. I had become a part of the block, and the block was a part of me.

Movin' out to Kendall ended up being another miserable transition for me because there was no more corner store, no more hangin' out, no more shootin' dice and doing dirt with the boys around the hood, and I was about to become like a fish out of water again. There was no more just runnin' over to school to play hoops. I missed all of that. It had become a part of me. And, of course, the homies—all of my friends—were back there. Everybody knew who I was, and I knew everybody.

Kendall was a brand new place, and I just felt way out of bounds. I was in a place that, first of all, was populated almost entirely by white people. No, I'm not talking Connecticut, California, or Swedish European white people; I'm talking about South Florida, Confederate State, Jeb Bush–ass white people. I'm talking a whole different breed. You gotta understand, I moved from Jamaica to Liberty City, so Kendall is not the type of racial breakdown I was used to seeing at all. In my Kendall school alone, you basically had 100 whites to 1 black, if you want to count it like that. This was not such a good feeling, and I was about to find out why.

First, I had to move from the peaceful Jamaican countryside to the contrast of Liberty City, Miami—a reality check I wasn't ready for. Then I had to move from the serious block out here to the burbs—another reality check I wasn't ready for. I was about to *consciously* face some redneck-ass racism for the first time in my life. My mother's act of moving us to this new neighborhood was supposed to be a way out, a way into a better kind of reality.

I remember the first time I went into the school—my new school in Kendall. As I'm walking out after the first day of school, somebody yells from a window, "Hey porch monkey!"

At first, I didn't really realize what was going on. I mean, in my mind, *What the hell is a porch monkey?*

It becomes crystal clear when he follows up with, "Yeah, I'm talkin' to you, nigger."

Wow, I think. *I definitely know what that means.*

Now if you think about this, you can easily see it's a bad combination. I'm still that dude from 22nd and 90 Street in Liberty City who don't take shit. So I'm desperately trying to see whose face this is yellin' from the fuckin' window. I just want to see his face 'cause I'm saying to myself, *I swear to God, when I see this face again I'mma punch it.*

I look. I look some more. I can't see too clearly who it is, so it's cool.

For now.

I go to school the next day. I'm still trying to adjust to this new life and new environment. I had already signed up to play trumpet in the band. My moms was trying to keep me at least a little musical 'cause I was all sports—and other things. When I walk into this band class, the room is packed. No open seats. I'm in a sea of white faces. Everybody's sitting down. And I'm not. I'm standing there without a seat. *Okay, fine, no problem,* I think. *I'll stand.* Class starts.

After a while, this dude gets up out of his seat and walks outside the class. I'm thinking to myself, *Finally, I can sit down.* I had been standing all morning. So I go and I sit down like Rosa Parks. Hell, my feet are hurtin' too, just like hers were. I sit. Again, *no problem.*

So I'm sitting there in class, and after a long minute the dude who got up and left walks back into the class from wherever. Next thing I know, he's tapping me on my shoulder. He says, "This is my seat."

Now wait a minute. He *touched* me. The fool tapped me on the shoulder. Okay. Obviously, I don't know anyone in this school, and obviously they don't know me—especially this dude.

So, it's starting to appear to me that he was expecting, in all that time he was gone, that I would continue to stand and wait for his dumb ass to come back and squat, rather than sit down in a clearly empty seat. Okay. Got it. Power struggle. I look up at him. He's looking at me. Since we're in a school, I figure I need to school his ass on what he's not understanding. So I say to him, "You got up, you went out, I sat down."

He looks at me, and clearly he isn't moved by this. So he fires it off again: "This is my seat."

Okay. Conflict. Finally, something I'm familiar with. I'm starting to feel at home. Obviously, this dude must want it.

So being the smart-ass that I can be sometimes, I get up out of the seat, pick the chair up off the floor, turn it over, then turn it every which way, and tell him, "I don't see your name on the seat."

He didn't like that.

He says, "Alright, cool . . . alright." Then he starts callin' me the "N" word. "Okay, nigger, we gonna see. We're gonna see, nigger."

So I'm like, *Blah, blah, blah, fuck you.* I wasn't trying to hear this fool. He walks out of the class again.

Now I'm back in the flow of class. Everything is cool. And before I know it, I see one white boy and three Spanish dudes standin' at the door. He's back. And he's tappin' on the glass, pointin' at me hard. Okay. I'm starting to feel more at home with each minute that goes by. So I get up. I get up because I come from a neighborhood where there's a shoot-out in my yard at seven years old, a neighborhood with crackheads, block riders, drug slangas, and killas. I mean . . . I'm used to this kind of shit. *What kind of beef these fools got for me?* I'm thinking to myself, *All y'all is soft.* I see the palm trees, the big houses and I think, *Y'all don't know what life is. These a counterfeit bunch of little sissies.* So he keeps tappin' on the glass, and I walk out the door to confront that shit head on.

So I'm standing there looking at ol' boy. He thinks he's strong now 'cause he squaded up on me. So the white boy asks, "Yeah, nigger, what are you gonna say now?"

So I ask, "What you wanna do? Y'all supposed to jump me?" They didn't have an answer, so I say, "Well, whatever. We can do it right now." Yo, for real, I'm ready to get it poppin'. I was already mad about that "porch monkey" shit, so I'm ready. "Let's fuckin' handle this," I say.

Alright, so now they realize that I ain't backing down. I'm standing in front of four mu'fuckas, telling them, "Listen. If y'all wanna fight, let's just go do it."

One of them finally says, "Nah, nah, nah, it's cool." And they squashed that beef. Fake prankster-ass wannabe gangstas. I find out later they have this lil' gang. Some bullshit. I didn't know anything about gangs, gang life, gang members, a gang supposed be coming for you, and all that stupid shit. They're throwin' up all kinds of fingers and supposed gang signs at me. I don't even know what all that shit means. It means nothin' to me. *Fuck you;* that was my attitude about it.

After this all went down, I head back to the hood and round up a couple of the boys. I let them know I'm having a beef and that we need to go sort it out. As you remember, I have some kids who don't fuckin' play . . . at all. Period. End of story. We were about to wake these lil' bustas up. So said, so done. Me and my riders roll out to Kendall. We pull up to The Townhomes of Kendall and go over to the apartment where I'm staying. My unit is ready.

Now listen, there was this chick living in the complex where I was staying, and boy, let me tell you about women: they're so beautiful but so dangerous. I'll have to go into that one another time. But listen, this chick in my complex is datin' one of the white dudes in this clique—this gang. And in between time, one of them had pulled a lil' gun on me with his cousin. Okay. Fine. It was nothin'. A little gunplay. Like I said, I'm at home with this.

So, the dude lives a couple of blocks away in another apartment complex. I walk over to his chick's spot and knock on her door. When she answers, I say, "Hey, yo, tell your boyfriend to come over."

"Why?" she asks.

"Because we're about to beat the shit out of him. That's why."

She was like, "Oh, for real?"

"Yeah. Call him up right now and tell him to come over," I say.

And she did as I told her; again, *so said, so done.* Trap set. He rolls up. He gets out. We split him. We beat the shit out of him. Done.

The next day, we hear that the leader of the gang is supposed to be looking for us now. Got it. *Why make him look?* Instead of waitin', we find out where the he lives and just drive the fuck over to his house. We walk into the yard, and I yell, "Alright, where you at?"

See, I think for them, they were into this whole facade of this gang life shit. I don't think they were used to seeing dudes that won't back down, no matter how many in the hell of them we were up against. And flashing a little gun was nothin' to me. We'd been dealing with gunplay since elementary school. They were living in one world, and we were coming from another.

The whole thing just wasn't matching up as far as how they were seeing it and what their expectations were. So at that point, they backed down and that whole beef was squashed. Not later. Immediately. They turned out to be some really nice kids. Everybody went and had their milk and cookies after that.

Seriously, though, I fought right through school. Right through. I didn't stop. I can't even lie to you. Being down in Kendall and being exposed to this life, it just didn't stop—especially once I got a partner in crime. I hooked up with this one cat (a good friend of mine to this day) named Tyson. He lives in Jamaica even now. But we got together as kids down there in Kendall and set it off. I feel sorry for those kids now.

See, I don't know if I was rebelling because I felt as though . . . okay, wait. How do I say this? I'm saying I was coming of age and I was starting to realize things. It's like I knew who my father was—I knew what he meant to the world because people would come up to me and tell me every day. They would tell me day in and day out. So the lights were really starting to cut on for me. It's inevitable when you get to a certain age.

My eyes were opening, and I was watching my family, lookin' at my brothers Ziggy and Stevie, my sister Cedella, and everybody else. Honestly, I'm watching them and they're living like kings and queens. Like *royalty*. And they should have been. Their father had been crowned a king. But I was also the seed of this man, and I'm in a situation that's not so pretty. It's a struggle. Always has been. The questions were finally dawning on me, like, "If my father is this person who has made so many millions, why am I living like this?" Those lights were cutting on. And so, as far as my childhood, I think that was why I was so bitter; I think that, subconsciously, this was why I lashed out so much and why I did a lot of the things I did in the way I did them. Maybe in some strange way this was my way of coping with it—or maybe my way of not coping with it. But whatever it was at that point, I knew I was a bitter child and I knew I was bitter for that reason. Heavy issues were growing and burning in the back of my head. And I think they were burning longer than I knew they were burning.

So I fought a lot. A lot. I fought right through middle school and high school. And it was through those years that I raised a lot of hell with my rider Tyson.

The way I hooked up with my homeboy Tyson was interesting. I'm living in Kendall now. And this dude is something. This dude, he walks into the school for the first time when I am in the seventh grade. He walks in all strong 'n shit. He steps up to a seventh grader, this dude named Ashley, and asks him, "Who is the baddest kid in the seventh grade?"

So Ashley says, "Ky-Mani."

Tyson asks, "Okay, so who's the baddest kid in the eighth grade?"

Ashley responds, "Ky-Mani."

So Tyson says to the kid, "Well, you tell Ky-Mani that I wanna fight him."

Listen. I don't know how this dude got my house number! To this day, I have no idea. But, this dude picks up a phone and calls me at frickin' home! *Home.* Wait a minute. And the lil' cat spouts off to me in a Jamaican accent.

"Yo, I heard you the baddest kid in the seventh grade and eighth grade," he said. "And I just wanna let you know that I'm in the school now and I'm the baddest kid."

I'm on the phone, saying, "Whaaa? For real? Okay, yeah, you got a lot of talk, buddy. We're gonna see about that 'cause I'll be at the school on Monday morning." *Wow.*

Now, all of this happens on a Friday. And on that Sunday, my mom goes over to a friend's house and brings me along for the ride. When we get there, the craziest thing happens. It just so happens that when we step into the house, there's a little dude I've never seen before sitting there. He's around my same age, but no biggie to me yet; it's just a dude. He doesn't know me, and I don't know him.

As we are all sitting there in this house, my mom naturally goes off to her space where all the adults are and I'm left in the room with the other kids. One of her friends has a daughter, and the other friend had a son—whose name is Tyson, but I don't know this at the time. And he doesn't know my name. It's all just waiting to happen.

So I'm sitting there with these kids, minding my business. And all of a sudden the young girl says to me, "This is my cousin, Tyson."

Okay. Now hold on. I know I've heard this name before. And I know this is not the dude trying to front me off on my home phone. Can't be. So I say to her, "Tyson?"

She looks at me strangely to see what I am finding so strange. I turn to the boy and ask, "What school you go to?" The name he says is the right school. So I say, "Yeah? I'm Ky-Mani."

He says, "Yeah?"

"Yeah!"

Now, Tyson is a skinny dude, and you know me, I always had a bit of body on me. We immediately and at the same time walk outside, and I'm tellin' him, "Man you don't want none of this."

The kid is woofin' it right back at me: "Man you don't want none of *this*."

The little girl runs outside and yells, "What y'all doin? Y'all ain't gon' fight. Y'all moms sittin' right in the house."

It all got squashed. It's so funny. Right at that point, me and him, we became cool—and are still cool to this very day. And from that point on, let me tell you, we're like a damned whirlwind in that school. A hurricane.

We. Fought. Right. Through. School. Nonstop.

The situation got so critical that I would be sitting in class and this dude Tyson would be in the lunch cafeteria havin' a fight. The kids knew we were buddies, so they would run to my class right away, tapping on my window to let me know that Tyson was having a fight. I would literally wait for the teacher to turn around or step to the chalkboard, and I would sneak out of class to go fight. It was chaos. All school year long. Back in the day it was *havoc season*.

So I went through a lot of that in my junior high days, and by the time high school came around, nothing had changed. It was the same thing: drama. The high school was a new spot. Nobody there knew where I was from or had any idea about my background. They only knew the Marley name and that I lived in Kendall. That was my reputation.

At this school, we had some lil' dudes who came from this area called Richmond Heights, which was a more urban environment similar to where I was from. But to me, they were still open. The area they were from was still some sub-urb living to me. So that's what that was.

So now I'm in high school. My rep out there is just that I'm the little Marley boy from Kendall, and blah, blah, blah. And everybody had whatever they had to say about it. Whatever.

I remember one of my first fights when I got to high school. I was leaving school one Friday. My mom came to pick me up that day. Now, as I'm walkin' out, this dude says to me, "Look at that punk ass goin' home wit his momma." I saw who it was. But my mom was there, so I kept my head straight. That was the only Friday of my life *ever* that I wanted to get back to school on Monday morning *so damn* bad.

Over the weekend I'm thinkin' about this shit. I mean the whole weekend its just tormenting me. That was just my spirit. That's just my personality. I wasn't taking shit from nobody. I just wasn't wired up that way. My moms told me since I was a wee lad, "Listen, once a dude start bullyin' you, and you don't correct that shit, it's gonna continue every day." That was policy. From jump street, I wasn't taking no shit. None.

When I got back to school on Monday, I was just waiting for an opportunity. I was outside on the patio at lunchtime with my girlfriend when he walked out. This was the moment I'd been waiting for. I say to my girlfriend, "Hold my books. I'm about to go knock this dude out and come back."

She says, "No you're not, no you're not."

The dude is now walking up the steps toward the second floor. I come up the steps around him and said, "Yeah, you remember me? I'm that punk ass that was goin' home with his mother."

He's carrying a book bag and starts to take the bag off, which was a very bad move. Mistake. When his book bag gets to right where his elbows are, of course, I pop him. He falls and I start to kick him. Immediately. This little girl comes up the back steps and says, "Oh my God. He's killin' him." So I stop. I think he got the message that I didn't appreciate his statement.

I go back into the lunchroom, trying to mind my business. I'm standin' up in the lunchroom doing whatever, and all of a sudden I start to get this little eerie feeling. I'm getting the feeling that I'm being surrounded. So I'm standin' up on the bench, and this dude jumps up on the bench next to me.

I say to him, "Is that punk ass on the steps supposed to be some kin to you?"

At this moment, I'm seeing all kinds of dudes looking at me just mean-muggin'.

The dude answers my question by saying, "Fuck, you don't talk to me."

I say, "Okay." I then realize I am being surrounded. "What y'all supposed to do? Y'all supposed to be jumpin' me?" They look. I say, "Alright. Alright. Don't go nowhere. All y'all stay right here. I'll be right back." I walk out.

So I was going to go call my brother Rohan, because at this time he's playing football at Palmetto. This is the brother who played for University of Miami. In high school, he was a riot too. He was already wild. He was knockin' dudes out left and right the same way. So, my initial idea was to call my big brother. But just as I was about to do that, something said to me, *Call your mother.*

So I call my mother. I wasn't calling her to come out; I just wanted to call her and give her some information, to soften the news she was gonna get later. I figured I'd tell her first, so she could hear it straight from me instead of the principal's office. It would lessen the ass-whoopin' I was gonna get from that strap she had when I got home.

So she picks up the phone and I say, "Mom, I just called to let you know I'm about to get suspended from school."

"For what?"

I tell her, "I just had a fight in the lunchroom. A bunch of dudes just surrounded me, and it seems like I'm about to get into another fight."

In dialect, she says, "I soon come," meaning she's on the way.

We live about fifteen to twenty minutes away, but I think by the time I hung the phone up, she was at the school. I head back toward the patio area, but I am still waiting to use the phone again to call my brother Rohan. While I'm waiting on the phone, my mother arrives and asks me what happened. I gives her the story about what happened that Friday and what the dude mouthed off about. I then tell her about what happen that day when I saw the dude. I tell her how I punched him in his mouth. I tell her about his homies surrounding me. She says, "Bring me to where they were surrounding you at." She starts walking toward the lunchroom, but I stop her.

"Whoa, whoa, you crazy, Ma? You can't do that." I discourage her from going in there because I know she wants to go in there defending. But by this time, she's upset.

She asks me to show her the dude I had the beef with. Our administration offices were in portables at the time, so I open the office door to this trailer and point to the dude who was originally talking all of the shit about how I'm a punk-ass momma's boy and what not. I'm thinking I'm in trouble because my mom didn't really play when it came to that strap. When I mess up, she's wearin' that belt out and bustin' my ass. I went through a lot of that too. So she looks over to where the shit-talking dude is sitting and asks, "Him?" She looks at me again, and says, "Him? Him? Ya should have broke him jaw!"

Wow. My moms is really, really upset by now because now she's thinking he's got all these people, friends, cousins, and all of them about to jump on one man. *Me.*

So anyway, I had been into the office, processed on my story and everything already. I was given a ten-day suspension from school.

At this point, my mom asks me, "Do you wanna go home?"

I figure I might as well since I just got suspended from school anyway.

She says, "No. You can't go home. If you go home, they're gonna think you're a punk and they'll never stop messin' with you."

I'm wearing a little necklace, a bracelet, and ring. That was the thing back then. She tells me to take off my jewelry and my shirt and to keep on my white tee; she then hands me a towel. I'll never forget it. She says, "Go back to school and don't come home and tell me that nobody beat you up. You hear me?"

I said, "Okay," and threw the towel over my shoulder.

Now mind you, I'm a star athlete on my football team. I'm junior varsity. First year of school, and I'm a star athlete. I play quarterback, I play running back, and when it came down to the nitty-gritty, I play some linebacker. I got a few trophies at home. Some of the dudes who were surrounding me were also on the football team. So I'm walkin' back to the lunchroom with pure fire in my eyes. The first one I see, I was gonna knock him out. So I walk up to the first dude. And the way I'm walking and the look in my eye lets him know that I mean business. You know when you see somebody like that. I walk back in the lunchroom with just the intention of *fighting* on my mind. In my mind, it was going to be a fight . . . period.

One of the dudes says, "Nah, Marley, man. That shit ain't even like that man. Nah, I had let them fools understand what was going down."

Blah, blah, blah, blah.

He says, "That shit all good, Marley."

And it was over. They squashed that. No problems after that. Except suspension.

So yeah, I've been through a lot. Some of it necessary. Some of it not. But all of it drama. Nonstop. You know, I reflect on it now at an older age, and it's clear to me that I'm here for a reason. I'm saying this because I've been through some things that got dudes right now doing twenty-odd, thirty-odd years. Some of their offenses are the same things that I did and got away with clean. Brawling. Street hustling. I've even had a lot of gunplay action. You name it. I can see now that nothing but grace has me where I am—especially as another memory comes to mind.

The craziest thing happened to me one Thanksgiving. I'm at the club. I'm probably about nineteen at this time. Me and a bunch of my rowdy-ass friends get into a brawl with a bunch of dudes. The usual, right?

Well, we decide that we'll go home, get strapped, and go back to the club. Great idea, right? As you can see, getting the dude off the block is one thing, but getting the block mentality out of the dude is another.

So one of my homeboys has a sawed-off shotgun. We roll back, pick it up, and throw it in the trunk of the car. That was the only weapon we had that night. There are about five of us in a two-door wrecked BMW. I've got an ounce of weed on me, and I'm smokin' heavy. We're a bad story waiting to happen.

We're rolling the streets of Miami back to the club. And as soon as we pull out and get to a stoplight, we get pulled over by the police. Here we go. Scenario: the car is cloudy as hell and there is nothing but thick, chronic smoke coming out. Strike #1. I mean, this is some real movie shit right here, for real.

A cop hops out of the patrol car. I've got an ounce of weed in the side door. Strike #2. On top of this, my license had been suspended, and I have no insurance because of this. Strike #3.

The cop comes to the driver's side. When he gets up to the window, he tries to keep us calm because he can see now that there are five dudes in the car. The smoke comes billowing out through the window into his face. Strike #4.

He says, "Oh, don't worry about that. I have friends who smoke."

I say, "Alright, cool."

Then he says, "Sit in the car for a little bit while I run your tag."

Obviously, I knew what that meant. I knew he's going back to the car to call for backup. We're from the city, so I know the routine. When you're outnumbered, you call for backup. Seen it a million times. And like clockwork, four more cars arrive on the scene. They're all filled with white boys. More good news.

So four of them come up to the car, and one asks me to step out. I step out of the car, and the cop asks me for my name, my license . . . and everything like that. I tell him my license was suspended. I hand him my suspended license and he asks, "Any relation?"

I say, "Yeah, Bob is my father."

He says, "Okay."

One of the other white boys, who must have been a

rookie because he went to high school with my brother Rohan, asks, "Is Rohan your big brother?"

I'm thinking, *Wow.* But I'm kind of skeptical about sayin' "yeah" because in high school my brother was sometimes very arrogant. He could be a real frickin' prick in high school, and I'm hoping this ain't somebody who he's got hatin' his guts. So I'm kind of timid about answering him.

Finally, I say, "Yeah."

He says, "Oh yeah, that guy is an awesome football player."

Relief. So I wait.

Finally, the first cop comes and says to me, "Alright. Here's what we're gonna do. I'm gonna write you a ticket, and then we're gonna put you on your way." He sits on the back of the car and writes me two tickets. He takes the bag of weed from me. *He'll probably keep that for himself,* I'm thinking. He then says to me, "Listen. I don't want to go inside of your car because I'm afraid of what else I might find in there. But before you go, just so I can say I searched you, pop your trunk open then just close it. I won't even look in it." Strike #5.

I say, "Okay, no problem officer."

I jump back out of the car fast. Now I know that the shotgun is there in the trunk sitting in plain view; if I open it, that's the first thing he's gonna see. I have a speaker in the trunk, and the shotgun is sitting right in front of the speaker.

But I have to move to the car with no hesitation. "Oh, no problem," I say. I pop the trunk. I pop that shit fast, too.

He looks. He says, "Oh. My. God." And then he tells me, "Step back away from the car please."

I step back away from the car. Now so far, they haven't taken anybody else from the vehicle. Everybody else is just sittin' down. I'm the only one who got out of the car. It's just me, the cops, and this sawed-off laying right in the back of my trunk. The man is perplexed. So he backs away and he asks me, "What is this?"

Okay. Let me tell you somethin'. Lookin' back at it now, this is how I know I'm blessed. Hear me, right now. I feel so, so, so blessed, like my life has some greater purpose. And I know that I have to find that purpose and make sure that I do what it is that I was sent here to do. I *know this* now. And it's moments like this one that make it all clear to me.

The cop? He pulls the gun out—out of the trunk. Now let me tell you somethin', right here. The gun? The gun is a frickin' police-issued shotgun. Strike #6. Police issued. Luckily they had peeled, scratched, and filed the damned serial number off! You hearing me?

So the cop pulls out the gun, and it's *sawed off*. Strike #7. He says, "Do you know that this is a mandatory five years just for having this gun sawed off like this?"

I say, "No, officer."

"Whose gun is it?" he asks.

I reply, "Officer, I do not know."

"You have to know. This gun is in the trunk of your car."

I tell him, "Yeah, officer, but I have more than one vehicle. Sometimes I lend my car out. My uncle will drive it, my cousin will drive it, my boy will drive it, or whoever. So really and truly, I don't know who placed that gun there."

I don't have another vehicle. So he looks me in my face and says, "Listen. You seem like a good kid, and I know you know whose gun this is. If it's not yours, it's gotta be one of your friend's that's in that car."

So I say it to him again, "Officer, I do not know whose gun that is."

He says, "Okay." He tells me to sit back on the trunk of the car. He and his boys get into a football huddle; they spend about two minutes talking.

He comes back to me and says, "Listen. Like I said, you seem like a good kid. I don't know what you're doin' with this, but whatever you were planning to do, you're gonna have to change that. What I want you to do right now is . . ."

He stops because, at this point, it is occurring to him that he hasn't checked the gun yet. *Shit.* So he yanks down on the pump and looks at me. Then he yanks down four or five more times. There ain't nothing but shells coming out. Strike #8. He looks to me and says, "Not only is it sawed off, but you're riding around with it in your trunk fully loaded."

I can tell I'm stressing this dude out. The man puts the gun back in my hand and says, "I don't care where you find it, but you find yourself a body of water right now, the second you drive off, and lose it. Right. Now."

When I get back in car, my boys are looking at me like I just walked on water. They're sitting there and they're just realizing that these South Florida white boys in uniform just let us go. Wait a minute. Not only did they not lock me up for the weed, they only wrote me two tickets. Plus they gave me back the gun and told me to get rid of it myself. My boys looking at me like, *What the . . . ? Kid, how the fuck did you do that?*

One homie says, "Man, I thought we was all goin' to jail tonight."

And with that, we drive off.

Now personally, that did a lot for race relations in my head. Barack and *that* right there. No joke. Somebody's watching over me.

Seventh Lesson Learned:

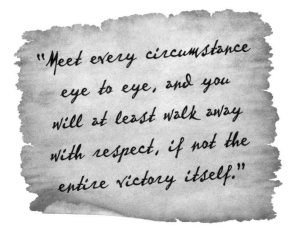

"Meet every circumstance eye to eye, and you will at least walk away with respect, if not the entire victory itself."

8

"You Neglected, Rejected and Ejected Me ... Still It's Only Love I Have"*

"DAMN! THAT'S WHERE YOU LIVE? YOUR DAD IS SUPPOSED TO BE SUCH AND SUCH, AND YOU LIVE IN THIS RAGGEDY-ASS HOUSE?" My father wasn't there, and I knew he wasn't there. He was gone. I was very aware of that. I didn't need little assholes pointing that fact out to me every five minutes. It didn't help.

The students at my elementary school all knew my last name and knew who my father was. And this occasionally

---

*From the Grammy-nominated, Many More Roads LP, by Ky-Mani Marley.

caused a few problems—at least for the kids. I can remember what happened the day one of the kids who attended my school came back to the block. He didn't live in my neighborhood. He was just there for a visit to the Ave. When we get to my street, we walk down the block, coming closer and closer to my house. At a certain point, we finally stop and he asks, "Where do you live?"

I point to our little board-house, showing him exactly where I live. It seems I had gotten used to what no one outside my neighborhood had quite gotten used to—the fact of who I was combined with the fact of where I lived.

He looks at my house. He studies it, in fact. The wood. The holes in it. I can see that he is shocked. I've seen that look before. He pauses. He thinks. He looks again. And finally it comes spewing out. "Damn! That's where you live? Your dad is supposed to be such and such, and you live in this raggedy-ass house?" *Wow. He had to say that, huh?* It had to be a big deal, didn't it? No. It didn't really. Not to me. But I could see that he wanted to make it one.

Well, it's unfortunate that we can all guess what happened the next day. We've all been that age, and we've all known kids that age. He wasn't going to handle this little bit of information with any decorum. His was too young to even know what the word meant. And unfortunately for him, so was I.

The dude lets loose all throughout the school and proceeds to tell everybody about my raggedy-ass house. He starts poppin' off at the mouth about my economic status and where I live with the raggedy this and the raggedy that . . . blah, blah, blah. And all I can do is keep hearing about it hour after hour, being racked with questions and stares from all of these kids.

After about that 1,000th question, I'm thinking, *Oh, it's about to be a problem.* The dude just keeps going. I keep hearing about it. He keeps mouthing off. And eventually, of course, he ends up getting into a huge-ass fight—with me. And with my fists. And I get suspended for that. For beating his ass. The usual, for me. After I'm done with him, I still have a raggedy-ass house and he ends up with a raggedy-ass mouth. I guess we're both in bad shape at this point. But at least his mouth was going to heal.

I couldn't hire any public relations people back then. I had to control my own public relations—if need be. My reality was just my reality. I, of course, missed my dad and wanted him around, like any child would, but mentally, I had moved on. Yes, we lived in the worst house for blocks, but I didn't want to think about that. I didn't have any interest in sittin' and cryin' over spilled milk. Naturally, I thought about it now and then, especially when I had to run up on lil' assholes, like the dude with the loose lips that ended up a little looser than what he wanted. But at the time, I couldn't focus on these little dramas and the reality that was sparking them. I was just focusing on getting back out on the block and doing what I felt I needed to do—

what I felt was necessary at that time. Hustlin'. No time for crying about it all.

My mom raised me with that warrior spirit, so I wasn't going to sit around and dwell on his absence or our conditions—at least not consciously. I just knew that my dad was no longer there. And I knew that all of this shit wouldn't be happening if he was here. It just wouldn't. Period. But the fact was that he wasn't here. And again, my reality was my reality. *Deal with it.* Right?

As the years went by, everything was insecure. Everything. Food, life, future. I didn't know what direction my young life was going to take. All I knew was the situation. And I knew that we were going to make the best out of the situation—and by *the best* I meant I was going to get us out of it one way or the other. *Out.* I used this all for my fire. I used it for my motivation. For my music. I don't know if it's right or wrong for me to say this, but if music wasn't it for me, and if I wasn't satisfied with a nine-to-five situation that paid nothing, I was going to end up robbing and stealing. Just like a lot of 'em. Period. I'm not alone. Only some of you can understand where I'm coming from because only some of you have been where I have been. The rest are civilians to what I'm talking about—civilians to the life I've lived. But I've seen life from both sides now. And I tell you, I'm understanding a few things.

I am not alone. Think about it. It's like the hip-hop movement: the rap game. It's kept a lot of hard, hungry, angry people out of your homes, out of your cars, and out of your face, 'cause it gave them the opportunity to do something more productive with their lives. Nobody is born wanting to hustle the corner, thug, rob, kill, and steal. Nobody. Negative circumstances produce negativity in humans if they get pushed to it. I'm no better because of my last name. Look at me. I'm the son of a king by DNA, but I grew up in the gutter by circumstance. I had to scrap, scrape, and struggle to live like the rest. It didn't matter who my father was. I grew up in the trap, the ghetto. I'm just like the millions who are out there—right now. I wanted to live. Survive. Just like you would if you were there. *Survival* is the instinct of life itself, and like I said before, if it meant selling all the fuckin' drugs in America, that's exactly what I would have done to make it out. That was my clear perspective about it. End of story. And one way or the other, and maybe even another, my mother was going to survive, my family was going to survive, and I was going to *make sure of that.* I was going to survive. I wasn't going to let the condition I was in tear me down or deter me from being or becoming what I could become. Neither was I going to let it mentally take me out of the game to keep me depressed or broken and away from what I could achieve in life. I was going to take the *nothing* I had and turn it into *something.*

When people are drowning, they will grab on to the closest thing to them so that they can help pull themselves up for air. This is what many people in these ghettos do. But I was going to do more. I was going to survive. Like many in these ghettos do, I was going to survive. And I was determined to get a successful life in whatever lane opened up for me. And if one didn't open, one was going to get carved out. This is how Anita raised me: never ever back down. Survive by any and all means necessary. No falling. No dying. We're coming up. Period. Judge me, hate me, love me, debate me. It's your choice. But it's so real, and real is exactly how I keep it. Why would anyone ask me to do anything else?

And listen, it's true. You don't have to wonder about what you've been wondering about this whole time. It's true. They knew. Yeah, the family knew. It wasn't like my mom and I were over here struggling in the States and it wasn't known by the other side of my family. My father's side . . . they knew. There were no secrets. And knowing that they knew this and didn't step in at any time, not even to say, "Here's a new pair of new sneakers," yes, that hurt. That shit hurt.

It. Hurt. Deeply so.

But I was at an age then that helped me not to focus on it. This was primarily because I had a lot of love on my mother's side of the family. It counterbalanced a lot of what was in me. Thanks be to Jah the Almighty. I had a lot of love. And with all that love, I kind of learned to overlook certain things. It helped keep the sting of it away for quite some time. I would hate to imagine what I would have become if that love wasn't there. I can't say that I'd be this productive member of society that I am today. I might be quite the opposite. Maybe I'd be somewhere trying to take from society because deep down inside I felt that society had taken something from me. Maybe I'd be in this same mind-state that so many millions are today. Isn't this the base psychology of the basic criminal, from carjacker to terrorist? Think about it.

The love that we kept alive in our Henlon circle has always made it sufficient for me, because even though we didn't have anything, it didn't feel like we didn't have anything. And this was purely because of who this Henlon family was to me. Like I said, *broke in the pocket don't mean broken in spirit*. At least it doesn't have to. We were survivors, and even if it was just some damned cabbage and rice for dinner, day in and day out, we ate. We still had something to eat, partner. We were going to eat. You hearin' me? But it's all true. It's just the way it was. And as I got a little older and I started reflecting on it all, I thought, *Wow*. It was a speechless moment. I couldn't even articulate what I was feeling, what was swirling inside of me. The hurt. The pain. The sadness. The rage. The disbelief. *I can't be seeing what I am finally allowing myself to see*. Maybe that kid from my elementary school was right the whole time. Maybe he just wanted to tell the world the wrong that was happening to me. Maybe he was taking on the cause that I hadn't yet found the strength to take up. And subsequently, he had to take the brunt of the pain that was always brooding somewhere inside me 'cause I just didn't know where to put it.

Like I said, for me, growing up Marley has had its double edge. It has brought me many blessings, including some of the highest joys I have ever felt. But it has also brought me some of the lowest lows I have ever been made to feel. And I would never want you to misunderstand exactly who I am. I want to make it all *completely* clear to you.

I love my Marley family. Period. I love them. I love *both* of my families. Every last member. Love them. I'm the type of man who reserves his deepest love and loyalty for family. It is my personal creed. For Ky-Mani, nothing feels better than family. And yes, we have traveled some extremely hard roads to get to where we are today, but we are here. And I *love* my family. We do still occasionally bump heads, fall out, make up, and have misunderstandings, but again, this family has my love. They have it in a way that is beyond their understanding and sometimes beyond my own. That is what it means to love unconditionally, and unconditionally is how I believe a family should love. The family should be the first and last place in the world where you find you are accepted for exactly who you are. No more, no less.

I don't want you to misread or twist up any of what I say. There's a bigger picture here that I am trying to bring to the surface. A bigger picture for us all.

When I'm around my brothers and my sisters, a feeling comes to me. It's a feeling that naturally can't be explained. It's like, my heart smiles. You know? It's like, my spirit is smiling. Everything on me and about me is literally smiling.

I feel a connection within that is unbelievable and undeniable. So what I want you to know is that I am like this always. My family could not stop this feeling I have about them even if they tried—each of them. I love them that much. I love them so much that I would fight and die for them. Each of them. I'm a soldier. It's how I was raised. And that's it. No questions necessary. Just tell me where, who, when, and how, and I'll get it done—together, we make solutions out of problems. And I would do this for them not because of who they have been for me or who they might be to me in the future. I would do this because of who they are. They are part of a man whom I love with every ounce of my being: my father. I would do this for each of them because each of them is a part of *him*—each of them is a part of me.

So when there is conflict between us, there is no wedge between us because I choose not to place one. I have my pains. I have my regrets about what happened, but I have this love—this undying love for my family. If this love hasn't changed already from the things that I have gone through, then it couldn't. I am the evidence of that. I'm trying to live by the code, not live by the past.

All my brothers and all my sisters have been there for me throughout a lot of my journey, just not so much in the start of it. But they definitely have been in my corner at later times in my life, and I want that known. I don't take that away. Their presence is felt with me consistently. I've learned a lot along the way from my brother Rohan, who was closest to me because he was also raised in Miami. I'm very close to Damian. I've learned so much, even musically, from my brothers Stephen and Ziggy. I mean, at the end of the day, we're just like any other family. We've been through some trials and tribulations. But no matter how disappointed I may be or get about certain things, the love is unconditional. That's just who I am. This is how I stand for family, and I want them to know that this is exactly how I want to be stood for.

I haven't written this book to speak any lies or to tell any stories; I'm not trying to create any ripples or cause any bruises—though my words might. I am here to share my reality and truth. I am here to tell my story and hopefully learn something from it upon reflection. I tell my story so that, upon reflection, my family will also learn something from it. I hope that others who struggle may take something from my story and find their own redemption by the virtue of reflection. There is good in the good and even good in the bad. And the telling of truth itself has a way of liberating and healing things that were hidden from the light. But it can't liberate or heal if it's kept in the darkness; I mean kept in darkness from you, from myself, or from my family. Truth will hurt at times. But ultimately, heal. We all need to tell it more often. Get it out. Feel it. Heal it. Get beyond it. Once we've completed this leg of the process, we can move on to what's new and what's possible in the business of loving each other on a higher level—the level of love that we all have come here to give and receive. What else have you come for?

Human is human. Love is love. And we all need a clear flow of it. The lies and hidden hurts that we hold kink up the flow until we let them out. Once we lift them from our systems, that pure love can flow again. It can flow when we detoxify our hearts of what we hold. Purge, and that purity returns. This is what I'm talking 'bout here. I'm not only sharing my story so that it can contribute something to me, my sisters, and my brothers; I'm sharing so that it may contribute to others and their own stories—their challenges at home, in their circles, and in their lives.

When it comes to my own family, I've experienced a lot of mixed emotions over the years. I'm sure you've done the same with your family. I've got sisters. And I've got brothers. We're all produced from the same father, but some of us have different mothers. This has given us a little drama over the years. My sisters are grown women now, and we brothers are grown men. And I know that a lot of the differences that my siblings and I have gone through over years were mainly instigated by our parents, that is, by our mothers. Having different mothers . . . you know how that goes. Conflict seems almost unavoidable. One group is raised to feel as though they're better than another group for whatever reason. And as children, we are taught many things, both directly or indirectly from the words, attitudes, and the simple energy of our parents. We all absorb and model the adults who have been around us the most. And we absorb this in ways we don't even understand. It's natural, whether good or bad. This happened to my siblings. This happened to me. And this created wedges between us that I'm sure none of us saw at the time. We were just reflecting who we were around most.

My heart, soul, and upbringing tell me that Rita Marley has had no love or joy over the fact of my creation for all of these years. In fact, my upbringing is the confirmed evidence of this. I have been touched by her disdain all these years—made to feel her feelings about my birth. And I know it is the same for any of the other children who were not born to her. I know how this affected *my* life. I know how much pain I have endured because of it. I know that these expressed ways and words of my father's wife may have affected many of my brothers and sisters and their ways of being toward me, whether consciously or subconsciously. How could it not? But knowing this has not eased the pain of it. Receiving venom from a direct source or from a surrogate makes no difference: the bite of the aggression is the same. The venom of it still courses my veins today, going from boiling to cold to boiling again, just looking for a way out. Just looking to heal.

Rita's not the only one. My mother played a part in this as well. The adults will go to war, and sometimes the only casualties are the children. When things got to a certain pain of financial hardship while I was growing up, my own mom would clearly state, "Oh, your brothers don't give a damn about you! Your brothers don't care about you!" And when you hear your mother saying that at that age, you can't help but believe it. I couldn't help but be affected, just like my brothers couldn't help but be affected by whatever their mother was saying about us. I can only imagine what they have had to absorb about me and any of us living outside of their immediate household.

So yeah, we went through those little times. And I can't directly point a strong finger at my older brothers for not seeing about me, because at that age and from that young, it's true that a lot of things were just motivated by our parents. I got that.

But we're grown men and women now. So why do we do what we do? Even now? What lingers? These are questions we need to face, because *it's not your mother and it is not mine.* We're grown. My mother can't influence me like that; I'm a grown man. Our decisions, moods, ways, and actions are now autonomous, right? We are self-governing, self-deciding, self-ruled. Are we not? If so, then what are we doing?

These are the questions that are going to get it done. Past, present, and future are laid out on the table. We've had our times. Some rough ones. But the future is held in our hands. What will we do with it?

I know the way things were for them in the past, and I definitely know how they were with me, because I felt that shit and I lived it. We're grown now and above this parental influence. All that is left now is the fact that we are the children of Robert "Bob" Marley, a musical and social icon for peace, for love, and for justice. We may not be connected through our mothers, but we are connected through our father and the mission of our father. I'm asking, *Where's the family in our family today?* I'm not talking about surface level. I'm talking about deep in our hearts. I want to know what lurks.

We haven't even scratched the surface of the potential that we have as a family, or as a force for change around the globe. Not even close. Sometimes it feels as though that support I have from my Marley family is conditional or that there is support only when I'm doing exactly what is expected of me by some members of my family. And everybody knows I'm the black sheep. I'm the bad boy of the family. So you won't find me too often doing what somebody else wants me to do—*just because.* That's like expecting your microwave to toast bread. That's outside the nature of that thing. And the whole *go along to get along,* conform to the norm philosophy is way outside the nature of me. I was born swimming upstream, so don't fault me for buckin' the current. It's naturally who I am.

It is true that I often don't feel support from my family creatively—like these days, when I branch off and decide I need to do some things on my own. And when I say "support," when it comes to a family like mine, it means a lot on myriad levels—because of the power my family members wield. It's not just like your brother coming to you, giving you a slap on the back, and saying, "Hey, I support you." My family is well established in my industry; my family members have ways in which they can lend support and cause an effect, and they have ways that they can make themselves felt in a vacuum of support. The impact of sentiment and attitudes happen on a huger level, for sure. But even just that slap on the back is worth something at times. I'd be happy for that if it were sincere and from love.

I have a creative family, fueled by the talents passed on to us by our dad. But a lot of our individual musical artistry just doesn't come out the same way because we came up in different ways, in totally different realities, in different atmospheres. And that's okay—at least with me. But maybe it is not so much with some of my siblings. Regardless of this, I want to feel that support, that love, that backing from all of my brothers, all my sisters, for one reason and one reason alone: we are family. Creative differences of directions and decisions should have no impact. We're still blood. We're still connected. Our DNA matches up. What I'm saying is this:

"So I feel that whatever it is I'm doing, musically or other, you're supposed to want to see the best of it. You're supposed to want me to bring out the best of it, and you're supposed to want to help bring out the best of it. And I'm supposed to want the same for you. That's family, friendship, neighbor, or whatever. You hearin' me?

"Now, if we're having issues just trying to achieve support from one another in the basic arena of our creative lives, then you know the other areas of our lives are having even greater challenges and issues. This is basic—love basics—and it's still not happening. I know we can do better than this.

"See, at the end of the day, I feel as though even if we're not all under the same umbrella creatively we can share the fruits of our labor. You can still be a part of my workforce, of my spirit, and my creativity. And I can lend the same to you. But like I stated, it seems as though when there's a perception that I'm not in the Marley camp creatively, so to speak, I'm pushed to the side. And I don't get that. I don't. I have to be honest. It's been a lot of little things. When I reflect on them, this madness kind of gets to me. And this is now. Should it be this way? No. Little political bullshit like this should never trump family or trump the fact that I am your brother. Should it? At least that's where I'm coming from. And honestly little petty shit like this, when we're supposed to be family, it hurts. It all makes me ask myself, *What are we doing?*"

The other day I went on to one of my brother's websites. It's crazy. All my brothers, we're on one another's sites and MySpace pages. I go on one of my brother's websites the other day and it's like, *For real? Wow. Damn, he took me down. He took me down? Off his site? C'mon.* Things like this, they're incredible. So again, *What are we doing?* We have our differences from time to time, but I thought to myself, *That's really fucking lame.* Was it so serious that this grown-ass man took me off of his little MySpace page? Little chaos like that has been nit-pickin' at my soul for quite some time, and I thought, *Wow, what is this? What are we becoming?*

But I'm the kind of person who sits back and observes. I take a lot of those little jabs and I don't say anything. I've been taking them all my life in one sense. And that's one of the reasons I felt as though I needed to go out on my own. *If I'm with you and you're not pushing for the best of my abilities, and the best of my success in the simplest of ways, then it all makes no sense.* It makes no sense. When I see little things like that happen, I realize, *Okay, you're my big brother, but you're not really being one to me.* Then I know that my back is not really had. I'm not covered.

That's the way it is with family sometimes, I guess. Passive-aggressiveness or aggression can come at you from places you least expect it or want it—especially when you're the black sheep like me. But I don't want to get used to that, just because it's the norm in a family. We've got to be there for one another on a whole new level. I'm calling out for this.

I do have my big brother Rohan, who always provides strong support and who I can go and talk to about everything. Ziggy is a person I can call up and talk to if I needed to, like all my brothers. I can call 'em all up and talk to 'em, but on the real, it's just strange at times. I don't know how you say it, but sometimes it feels like a close-far relationship. It's the oddest thing.

When we're together, we have the best time. I mean . . . I really have the best time of my life. The *best*. But then the miniscule stupid shit that I can't seem to figure out happens in between. And as miniscule as it is, it tears me up on the inside because I know that the small comes from something larger that is going unsaid. At times I feel like some in the family have moments where they thrive off of people being dependent—or people being in a situation where they might be in need of them. And then they might think, *Okay, he can't progress without us.* This is truthfully the type of political drama I'm seeing, instead of them saying, "Well damn he's doin' great, so let's give him a push so he won't need us." That's love right there. Not that other. Not that other petty MySpace page–type move. I don't get that. And to be honest with you, I've never really talked to that brother about it. You can say it's wrong of me, but I thought, Hey. *You're a grown man. You know exactly what you're doing.* I know when I'm doing right and wrong. I don't need anybody to tell me. And if I'm doing somebody and injustice, I know it's an injustice. There's no way you can be doing an injustice and you feel as though it's justified. If you have an internal conscious, it'll tell you straight out when you're doing something wrong. Then you make your decisions from there. You decide to go with *the right*, or you decide to go with *the wrong*. We all have that inside, that barometer. And we read it how we want to read it. At this point, all of my siblings—brothers and sisters—we all know what we want out of life. The same thing they want for themselves and their children is what I want for myself and my children. So we make our decisions. And if a man is doing anything to short me of that, I'm quite sure he knows it. It's these kinds of petty dramatics that just don't sit right with me. Period.

Let's keep this totally real—of course, it's obvious that none of this is about a little Internet page pettiness, any creative or promotional lack of support, or whatever. Those things are nothing. This is about what those things point to going on deep under the surface. You know? Family politics can be a straight bitch. It can flow deep. And it can cut deep.

You have to understand what I'm calling *family politics*. It was family politics that gave me all of the growing-up experiences I have detailed in this book. Every one of them. That's where they flowed from. That's real. And that ain't anything on the scale of petty, small, or miniscule 'cause you see the way it touched our lives—my mother and I. The politics? As small and petty as it is and can be, it can also be *huge*. The impact and ramifications can be massive. Family politics can turn into life-and-death situations, like it did for me. Politics can be like waving a weapon in someone's face because it can threaten the welfare of someone's life in the exact same way. Whatever it all is, I know that it is not respectful to my father. It's not respectful to what he gave the energy of his life for.

Growing up struggling, I had to watch when my brothers used to come up from Jamaica to Miami and shop and spend money lavishly. I'd think, *Okay. If you have it, then go ahead and do it.* But I'd also think, *A lot of that money is also my father's money.* And I had to sit under the pressure of watching this—living at home with nothing, cutting cookies up into rocks to sell to crackheads on my corner. *And I gotta live through all of this because my mother wasn't married to my father, and your mother was? Is that right? Because my mother wasn't married to my father and your mother was, does that make me less of a Marley? I'm not adopted. I'm not adopted by your mother, my mother, or my father.* I'm not an adopted child, but for so much of my life I've had to feel like one even though I'm from the same DNA. *I'm from the same testicular sac that we all came from. Period. If you cut me, I bleed Bob Marley's blood, just like you do.* This man's blood is flowing though my veins and their veins right now, in exact and equal measure. So what's the deal? What did I do, other than be born? Nothing. Yeah, these have been my feelings and confusion on the matter of, *How could it all go down like this?*

I remember one time I saw my mom *really* upset. My father had passed away, and there was a big-ass fight going on with the estate and money was being reported stolen from my father's wife, Rita. There was talk about documents that were allegedly forged to control property, and all kinds of different things were happening around the world in different states and different countries related to resources that were supposed to be those my father would leave to the children. But things were being taken and going in another direction. It was drama.

Rita Marley and even Chris Blackwell of Island Records were generating a lot of drama around the property and monetary holdings of my father. You know how it is when a wealthy man dies: people lose their minds, and wolves come out of sheep's clothing. I can even remember one time when I saw my mom completely upset. I asked, "What's goin' on?"

She let me know that somebody from the estate (whether it was a lawyer or somebody else, I don't know) was responsible for writing a letter saying some outrageous things, including statements that I am not my father's child. Madness. My mom told me that she had written them back and let them know the dates, times, and full details of the entire sexual act! *Laughing*. You know my mom. Anita don't play. At all.

It was not like any true paternal question lingered as to how I came about or whom I belonged to. Even when I was back in Jamaica, right after my pops had passed away, the family used to travel through the country and they would sometimes stop and see me—not too often, but maybe twice in a year. They'd come to my little town, or I'd go to Kingston and stay for a week or two and then I'd come back home to where we lived. So my paternity must have been acknowledged. These were clearly my brothers and sisters. We would play together and eat together. We knew one another the whole time we were growing up. It wasn't like I was this kid who just showed up on the doorstep one day. So that couldn't be a justification for my mom and I being financially cut off, as if I died when my father died.

And let me tell you, it was crazy. I've told you about my living conditions growing up, so you know that there was no money coming in from *that* way. But when I would visit my siblings, it was like night and day. My brothers were stayin' where my dad stayed, naturally. So that house was a very big house. That house was three stories, had a pool . . . you name it. They lived on the top of the hill. Everything you could want in the house, it was there. Rehearsal room, gym, different bedrooms, a farm, all kinds of shit; and I'd be coming back home from two weeks of helpers, cooks, gardeners, and a lawn man to bathing and cooking outside in our front yard in Falmouth. It was crazy.

As a child, I just didn't think about that so much. I wasn't conscious of it. I only thought about it when I became an adult and started reflecting back on my life, thinking: *Whoa, wait a minute, hold on, what the hell?* But as a child I didn't think about that. The reason was my family at home—and that little country, Jamaica, where there was so much warmth. I didn't feel as though I was missing anything. We were living in a little wooden shack, but it was a comfortable house. We were bathing outside, but so was my entire family. We were cooking outside over a hot-coal stove, but that's what I was used to. Those types of poor environments didn't bother me like that because I was raised in them from birth until I was eighteen years of age.

I was in it, and so was everybody else around me in my neighborhoods in Jamaica and Miami. That's what the people around me went through. So for me, that was normal life. You go and experience something else and, yes, it's nice, but still, when I got back, this was the routine. It wasn't consciously bothering me yet. Not yet. In that little house in Jamaica, I was loved.

When you are a child, you can't clearly work out in your mind when injustices are being paid to you, because you just don't know—you don't have the experience to know. That's why, in other circumstances, little kids are often preyed on by adults. Because most of the time, kids won't even know what just happened. It doesn't hit them until they become adults and they think back to those times. So this was nothing for me at the time.

But when I became of age and I started to open my consciousness, I would reflect upon my life and think, *Wow. You're the son of a king, and you know this because people stop and tell you all of the time. So, how the hell was it possible for you to live through all of the mayhem you just lived through?*

It hit me like a wall of bricks.

Today, I can go anywhere in the world and see Bob Marley memorabilia somewhere. I've met people who don't speak one word of English but can sing every last one of my dad's songs word for word—per-fect-ly. So when I see things like that and then I reflect on my life, I think, *How was this shit possible?*

I was growing up, and I was wising up. Even if my mom and I were only getting a damn $300 to $400 a month, that shit would have been great for us and would have made all of the difference. At least we would have had that to look forward to. It was a multi-multi-multi-million-dollar estate. And nobody could ask if I needed a book bag? Something went wrong here. Very wrong.

As I was getting older, I started to hear about the estate settling on some of the court issues. I didn't know a lot about what was going on behind the scenes with the legal proceedings. I was still a kid, hangin' with my friends and hustlin' the block. I wasn't trying to deal with all of that. But I started hearing word that maybe some payout would finally be coming to me when I turned eighteen as my part of the estate settlement. I think I was sixteen or seventeen when I was hearing about this. It was all still kind of irrelevant for me, because some money tomorrow wasn't going to feed us today. So I was still on the street doing my thing: slangin', smashin' and grabbin', breakin', entering, boostin', whatever—you name it; I did it. I touched on damn near everything in hood life. Hell, I didn't even know if I was going to live that damned long to see some money. So *whatever.*

But I made it. I made it to eighteen. And when I finally turned eighteen, things began to shift. Suddenly there seemed to be this great interest and love or some feelings for me that I hadn't felt before. My family was showing me some level of love that I just couldn't explain. So I was getting a little confused, but I was flowing with it—and plus it was my time. It was my time to get this payment. I was finally going to get this lump sum of money, my part of my father's estate, that would get us up out of the struggle and my momma off the damn bus or the jitney so that we could wake up a little more peaceful in the morning without stressing over what would come next. It was good news. We had to go through hell to get to this point, but we had arrived at this day. It's all good.

The day had come, and we were ready to move forward. Finally, I was told by the estate, "Okay, you can have this lump sum of money. But if you take the lump sum of money, you're going to have to invest it all back into the estate in full. And we will give you (something like) three g's a month and a 60k payout for your bank account to start." Looking back, that's some old monkey money if you ask me. Then I was told, "If you choose *not* to invest the full amount back into the estate, you can no longer be a part of the estate," meaning its earnings.

Okay. Wow. So here I am. I didn't know the ins and outs of the estate business. I didn't know what to expect. All I knew was the situation that I was in before. Period. And then I was listening to my mother's views on it all, which wasn't always the correct teaching because it was her emotions at the time and how she felt about all that had happened up until this point. That's understandable. But I was the one who had a decision to make since I was the one cornered with these options.

So I looked at everything. I looked at my situation. I looked at my past. I looked at my grandma, my mom, and her family—all the hardships I'd been through, saw my mother go through, and saw everybody else around me go through. Then, I looked at my brothers and my sisters, who were talking about this money and putting it back. I'm saying, *For real. What would you do?*

I heard all of these voices and concerns in my head, and I thought, *Whoa. So if I don't give this money right back to you, that you just gave to me after all these years, now I'm no longer a part of the estate like I'm no longer a son of my own dad?* How could I no longer be a part of an estate whose earnings were based on my father's work, legacy, and intellectual properties? All of them could keep living on my father's earnings, but I couldn't? How does that work? And they wanted it *all* back—not half, not a quarter, all. Those were my options. And how was I supposed to trust that, if I gave all this money back, I would be taken care of in the future when I wasn't taken care of all of those years, with nothing? How would I know that my family was going to take care of me like they were telling me they would when for eighteen years, coming to this point, they were never there? What would make me trust that if I invested this money, all they were sayin' was gonna work out? Was I supposed to feel easy about doing this after all these years of nobody coming to check and see whether I needed shoes, socks, or a book bag for school? Really? Yeah. It was crazy.

My mom was naturally telling me, "You can't give it back. You have to keep it." I know she was scared. And I'm figuring, at this point, she must have some knowledge of what was going on and a reason for telling me to do that. Plus the voices were running down to me on the other side that this pay-it-back option wasn't coming with any paperwork—meaning I just had people talking to me about something that I was supposed to just take at face value.

There was no security in a decision like that for me. So I decided I was not going to do that. I was just going to take my share out of it. I kept the money. I didn't reinvest or give all the money back that they had just handed to me—which was what they wanted to me to do. But, that's okay. It just wasn't goin' down like that. And that caused a little bit of friction. Okay, maybe a lot. Those involved got hot. They all were upset with me, and I thought, *Wow. Is it really like this?* I thought this was supposed to be an "option" of my choosing, but apparently it was not. Apparently to some of them, there was only one *right* option, and I didn't pick it. So it was a little rough riding for a minute.

I remember calling my big brother Stephen after it happened, wanting to explain my decision or at least be open to hearing what I could be missing from the other side. I called him so that he could give me good reasoning or talk to me sensibly and help me understand what was going on. If his argument made sense to me, then it was no issue for me to reinvest the money. But when I called him, his girlfriend at the time answered. I asked for him, and she said to him, "Ky-Mani's on the phone for you." I heard him in the background tell her (and I knew he was sitting right there), "Tell him I'm not here." I thought, *Okay, cool. Got it.* I hung up the phone. That was that. When he decided not to speak to me, not to have a conversation about it with me, that was the nail in the coffin right there.

I had brothers and sisters who were upset with me, and they stopped talking to me. Period. I couldn't believe this. My perspective about it was, *Here you are telling me to return this money. But there you have been for your entire frickin' life spending money like there's no tomorrow. And the money you're spending, it's not like that's all money that you went out and earned on your own; a lot of it is still "our" father's money. So now, you can't be upset with me because for the first time I'm gonna be able to experience life a little differently—and this is something that you have been doing all along.*

But, I was shut down. Nobody would talk to me. I went without talking to my brothers for a good five to six years. This was after years of not seeing them throughout a big chunk of my youth, and only in later years finally seeing them more often over summers and whatnot. But everybody was upset over my decision about the money and mad with me. I thought, *C'mon you dudes been sleeping with millions all the long and here I am suffering, and you never came along and said here's a shirt for school or something to just brighten up my frickin' day, and so now I take the money that is allotted to me and now everybody's upset.* I started thinking, *What the hell?*

I was getting my dose of it: family politics. I was shut down. We didn't talk. And back then it didn't affect me too much because I wasn't raised in the same house with them. There wasn't this deep connection that had been established, nurtured, and then broken up. But it definitely touched up on me a bit that it was all going down like that. I caught a feeling on it; it hurt, although that wasn't going to break me. It couldn't ever approach that.

I was used to just being in the streets with my homies. That was my family. I was used to just having my mom, my grandma, my uncle, my cousins, and whatnot. That was my family. So it wasn't taking anything away that had. I guess nobody thought about that. They never thought, *How can we freeze a dude out that was already frozen out for years? What? Refreeze him?* My life was already filled with the coldness of those streets. At that time, I was in a totally different space. I was made so hard at that time in my life, nothing could have broken me—violence, jail, bullets, death. I was ready for anything from life. I had just come from living for years in a place where anything was possible, and so had everybody around me. But it is crazy now to think about the amount of time that went by, all that time of not talking to my siblings.

That little drama continued for quite some time. We did eventually kind of patch things up, and we tried to get it all together again. We got it back to the whole family vibe, back to where it should have always been. There was reconciliation. I was older. They were older.

By this time, I was launched into my recording career and really building a stake for myself in this music thing. We were getting it together, doing our Marley Show together, performing, and the whole business. It was what it was, the ups and downs. Things were good for a moment.

Then I saw the little separation return. The distance vibe came over it all again after I decided to sign my deal with Vox. My brother was a little upset with me. And maybe with some of this, too, I helped prolong this situation. So, I spoke to him about it and told him how I felt, and he said what he said. He was saying, "You don't understand," "We're still there," and things like that. And I was hearing him—on the surface. But honestly, for me the vibe just didn't feel . . . clean. It didn't feel clear. I was hearing him say what he was saying, and it sounded good and felt good at the time, but somewhere it just didn't sit right with me. The authenticity of it. But, I think that maybe if I would have taken it for what he said and just kept in touch, really pushed the issue, and went there with it, maybe then it would be a little better than what it is now.

But you know, keeping it all one hundred, keeping it all real, I just like when it's a two-way street. I feel that if you're trying to hold it down and be a good friend toward me while at the same time I'm still being an asshole toward you, well, that relationship is just naturally not going to work. I like a two-way street where we're both in the same frame of mind, trying to put some effort into this to make things work. So I was thinking, *Okay, you're telling me you're there. But you're turning your back to me while telling me you're there.* It's back to that far-close drama again. Nothing was matching up, word for actions. I was not feeling the real in that. But that's how it always seemed to be with me. Near but far, brother but broke, love your music but not so much. Black sheep, baby. Every family has to have one.

I go it alone a lot because that's how I came up . . . on my own. I didn't really have any choice. So that comes off as a rebel a lot, no doubt. But that's just Ky-Mani being Ky-Mani. I like staying as close as I can with my brothers and my family, but as far as my music, I just do me. If I were to do anything other than that, then what would I really be doing? Music is an expression from one's soul, and I can't express my music from what's in another man's soul. It's crazy for someone to expect that from me, and I'd be crazy to expect that from another man. *Me can know no man soul but mah own, yah mon?* I'm real. I don't know how to be anything but that.

I cannot live a life that someone else wants me to live, especially when I'm cut from such a different cloth. I only get to live this thing one time, so I have to do this my way and in the way that makes me happy. The same goes for you. What would you look like living the life that Jah Almighty gave you and you alone but living that life on someone else's terms and vision? If you do that, God just wasted a lifetime, giving it to you when you're just going to give it away to another man's vision. What's the use of two of you if the two of you can only think and do one way? That makes one of you unnecessary. You're the only one being pulled from that womb in the beginning and the only one being thrown in that pine box at the end. You better make sure that the time you spend between is worth it to you. Feel me on this. If living my life and trying to do what makes me happy while I'm here on Earth turns me into a black sheep, fuck it. I'll be that. I'll be the black sheep. But to my siblings I would say, "I'm still your family. Love me like that 'cause I already love you like that."

I know the person I am and what my family truly means to me, and I know what I'm willing to do for family if called to duty. When these sentiments are seemingly not reciprocated, it hurts me to the heart. Just being real with this. I was raised with unit thinking. We were "one." So when some small things go down, I say, "First of all, how could this be this way? I could never think of doing that to you." But that's that black sheep mandate, a mandate where I have to be the one to get cold shouldered at times, regardless of whether I would show you the same treatment or not.

I have to understand, they say seven brothers, seven minds. Nothing is new under the face of the sun. However, there should be something at the base of all of our minds that ties us together. Individual minds can prevail but with a singular principle of family unity at the base, can't they? Isn't this the way it should be? This is unit thinking where individuality can still be respected. Damned, that's kind of the basis of this whole free society isn't it? If it is not in reality, at least it is by the concept. There can still be unity without suppression, squashing, or alienation of individuality. It is possible. Then what's up inside our family? I think there's a lot that's not being talked about.

This cold war that gets waged on the inside of our family between the so-called legitimate and the somehow perceived illegitimate sibling is madness. It's ignorance, and it is so not our father. *That* is someone else. And that shit motivates me because sometimes how I see it as, *Oh, I'm not supposed to win. Okay. I'm going to push even more.* And push to the top. "Never ever back down" is how I was raised. Challenge is no stranger to me. And there is no fear of challenge. But there is so much challenge out here in life that the last place you want to see it come from is inside of your family, whether it is a cold war or a hot one. Family, friendships, and marriage should be catapults for the individual, not something to potentially harm them, hold them back, or reprimand them for individual freedom of expression.

"Of course, if you see me doing wrong, then you can guide me, but you can't cheat me on my journey because I'm on my own journey and I'm takin' the ride I wanna take. I wouldn't do you like that. Don't do me. Just talk to me and express your view and wisdom on it. Don't give me a cold war. I'm a big boy; I can take it. I can take what you have to say or any disapproval. Don't cold-shoulder me. Give me communication. Not politics.

"I'm supposed to be able, no matter what, to come talk to you about anything. If the love we have is real, it's supposed to be a love where you can hear me under any situation. If the love we have is real, it's supposed to be a love where I can hear you under any situation. Because when it's real, it's that strong. If you're my sister or my brother, and there's real love, I'm supposed be able to come to you and say, 'Hey, you kind of fucked up in that situation over there. And this over here with such and such was really fucked up too.' You feelin' me? And you're supposed to be able to take that. You're supposed to be able to take that, no matter how upset you are—and take it away to yourself and think about it. And then you think to yourself, *Okay. Maybe I did fuck up. But we're gonna move on. We're not gonna let that cause any animosity between us, because the bottom line is we're still blood.*

"This applies vice versa. If I do something wrong, you're supposed to be able to come to me and say, 'Hey, Ky-Mani. You fucked up.' I'm supposed to come back and say, 'You know what? Yeah, I apologize. I don't know what the fuck I was thinking then, but I love you.' Understand what I'm sayin'? And we keep it moving. That's the code. That's what family is all about. Loving, living, healing, laughing, and keeping it moving. Family. You don't let that poison take root and start to grow in you. We gotta learn how to communicate. Freely.

"Up to this point, I have tried to not get involved with the politics I've seen around me. I guess I'm in it now. But I'm involving myself now not as an effort to join in the madness but as a call to eradicate the madness. And even this call may tear us further apart, or it may bring us closer together. It's a jump ball. But if there is love, I think it'll bring us closer together 'cause I'm telling you raw truth about the feelings. I ain't dressing it up. Truth is supposed to set us free, liberate us, and heal us like an herb to a wound. Many influences are at play here, and I pray that the mind, heart, and spirit of our father comes over it all so that a new outcome can be produced for us—above the influence or mind-state that had gripped us for too many years.

"Growing up with nine people under a small roof, I have this concept of family as an unbreakable unit. It's just the example that I was raised with. One for all, baby. Period. And this is even the philosophy and example of our father, no? This other way is not the example set by our father. I'm not in love with that. There should not be any outcasts in our family or even anyone who is made to feel that way. There shouldn't be siblings who get a monthly check from the estate of our father but at the same time are made to feel the compensation is more like a favor than what a man or woman is rightfully and lovingly entitled to as an extended part of that man's (Bob Marley's) anatomy and soul. That shouldn't happen. That's not our father's spirit. That's not our father's philosophy. The Gong's message is 'One Love.' Not one love for you and then one love for me. It's one love for all. Worldwide. Humanity. And I can't spread his message across the world if I can't spread it first in our own house. Hear me, right now. If you love this man and what he stood for, hear me.

"I've said a lot here. And there is a lot that I have not said in this open forum and have left for us to discuss in intimacy. And again, it could tear us farther apart or it could bring us closer. But there are two reasons that I have said what I have said. #1—It is a part of the fabric of my story. #2—I want something better from us as a family. Period. I want this for us, and I want this for our dad.

"See, this has not been the rantin' and cussin' of a madman bitter about money. *No, mon. Fah dem dah see mah heart, dem jus know.* This here—this conversation here—is not even about *money*; it never has been. This is about *love.* I tell you, I grew up a *wealthy* boy because I grew up in the lyrics of my beloved father—*our dad.* I was surrounded by *one love.* And this conversation that I am offering right here is a call to action—a call to the embodiment of this one love, the love that our father gave the energy of his entire lifetime to establish in the world. I'm calling us up to that mission, family. I'm calling for this love to heal the strains in our family first and then the world—*wide.*"

I'm telling you. I have seen this life from both sides now: rich and poor. Money is just something to help you live, but love is what you live for. And if you're living just for money, you will find that once you get it, and you have it without love, you're a poor man all over again.

I want us to stand up as a family, as individuals, and be about the work of our father, spreading love to the forgotten and the castaways of this world. I want my family to be a force for this message.

My final message to all my siblings is this, "I could never *have* while you *have not.*" I literally grew up sharing and eating from the same pot with nine people, drinking from the same mug with nine people. If I have it, they have it. And honestly, this is what I had never understood about my siblings before. Because it was not the way I was raised, and I never considered it the way of our father. But that was then, and this is something that I want you to understand about me. I love my family. I really do. And if they call me, I am there for them. And in my heart, I hope that they would be there for me. Like our dad would want us to be.

To my brothers specifically, I say, "We are all men with our own children and aspirations. We all need to nourish that and help one another with our passions in life, to help one another stand strong. No branch is more significant than the other. The only significance is the trunk of the tree that holds us up, and that is our father. Know that.

"Our grandmother Cedella used to tell me that nothing made our father happier than to see all of his children gathered together. I know that he's here still. It may not be in the flesh, but it is definitely in the spirit. I want us all to carry on the legacy and life in a way that would be pleasing and satisfying to him. I can't say that everything that we do is going to be satisfying to him, but I can say that we can try.

"I don't want any of my family to worry about the past and all the things that I have said here. It is just the past. It is just my story. The past is even the last breath you have just breathed. It can go away that easy. Let it go. So will I. I know and accept that Ky-Mani had a different path to walk, a different destiny to fulfill. Maybe I got a little hollowed out in life, to become a better instrument of Jah. And after a while, after some years, it all comes full circle. I'm alright. But it hasn't been easy. It's always been a fight. It's been a constant fight for me from the moment I've known myself to the moment I give you these words. But for me, I just roll with the punches and always take good out of bad. And go on."

If it happened, it was meant. And I know now that I was born to touch lives like our father touched lives—and I couldn't touch those lives had I not been touched by what touches them today. I couldn't sing to their pain if I hadn't felt it. Families have ups, downs, ins, outs, joys, pains, misunderstandings, and then love. That's the human condition. But I can't front on the fact that I love my family with my all, and if it came down to it, *I know* that they're going to stand in my corner.

"Ziggy, Stephen, Robert, Rohan, Julian, Damian, Cedella, Karen, Stephanie, Sharon, Makeda: I love you. The past is the past. But the future is the future. It is ours to write. And I want a better one for us. For all of us. And for all of our children. We can do better. I know we can. We can make it *irie*. I'm committed to this. And I invite you to this commitment with me. I wanna see him smiling down on us. Don't you?"

Dear Dad ...

We *irie*.

DEAR DAD (Lyrics by Ky-Mani Marley)

Dear God,

I have a letter here from me to Dad,

and I want you to know it might be a little sad.

(Here it goes)

Dear Dad, I really didn't get to know you.

Sometimes I sit and wonder and it makes me blue.

But there is one memory that stays on the back of my mind.

And this memory got me thinking 'bout you all the time.

Oh, Pa, I swear we miss you so.

And I wish that you were here to see your boys grow.

In case you are wondering, Mommy she's doing fine.

And she tells me stories 'bout you Papa all the time.

So when I'm down and out, lonely or just feeling blue.

All I do is think of you.

The thoughts alone erase my fears and dry my tears.

I'm just writing to let you know someone cares.

Daddy, I love you, I love you, really, really love you.

Daddy, I miss you, I miss you, and I know my brothers and sisters do too.

And I know you gave your love to the people.

And some of whom you thought you can trust, they deceive you.

But betrayal brings another day.

At least that's what my mother say.

And when I'm thru I'll place this letter in the Bible.

And I'm gone to pray to Jah to send his disciple.

To deliver you this letter.

It will make me feel better.

Daddy, I love you, I love you, really, really love you.

Daddy, I miss you, I miss you, and I know my brothers and sisters do too.

Eighth Lesson Learned:

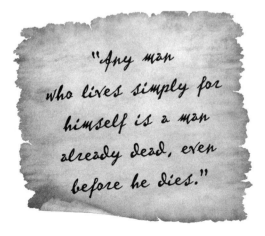

"Any man who lives simply for himself is a man already dead, even before he dies."

9

Many Mansions in My Father's House

I DIDN'T DECIDE TO DO MUSIC. This was my destiny. It was written. Even though I was born as the son of a musical icon, being a musician couldn't have been any further from my mind than it was. My interests as a young lad coming up were completely opposing. I was a star athlete in high school with an obsession for football and an obsession for soccer going back to when I was five years old. Music just wasn't it, not for me. Although my mother would attempt to get me guitar lessons and keep me in a school band, the lessons seemed like more of a punishment than an interest—music was something taking my time away from the activity and fun of sports. And since I didn't grow up in the Marley household, I didn't grow up seeing my brothers in rehearsals every day or hanging out with them in studios or on tour. That's not how my time was spent. It just wasn't like that for me.

Growing up, my mind was on other things. Serious things. Survival. Runnin' the street. Hustlin' the corner. Gettin' money. Beefin'. Music was never even something I gave a passing thought about doing. For some people, it's hard to imagine me coming up as the son of Bob Marley and not wanting to be involved with music. But that was me. Music was something that just came into my life and took me over, more and more. And as it did, I just let it. I let it flow. Why not? I wasn't doing much of anything else, just getting in trouble. And what started out as joking around in a friend's basement on his sound system turned into one opportunity, then another, and then another. One door would lead to another door, which would lead to another. And before I knew it, I was on the stage at the Midem Music Conference in Miami before a bidding war would jump off to sign me. It was nothing I dreamed about or even chased; it just came knocking. All I did was answer, walk, and follow it—and it became clearer with every day that went by. This was written. This was my destiny.

I now know this, whereas maybe I used to guess about this in the early days of my starting out. I now know that this is part of why I'm here—why I'm still living today. And when I realize that, I start to focus intensely, especially on the album I'm working on now. It is a whole new level of consciousness that I'm bringing to my music. I'm doing this from the writing, the composing, the style, and the genre mix to the business of it. I can feel my father's spirit with it.

When I first started this career, it was more of a ride and I was just trying to see where it would take me. But now I see my purpose, and I'm fully in the driver's seat of this thing, taking it where I want it to go. I'm really working, creating and recording at a new level for myself and my fans; I owe them the best of me both musically and lyrically. I want to make sure that when people listen to my music, they're not just hearing a beat and some rhyming words over the top. They can actually take something away from this. I want them to take something away they can keep for life. That's where I am now.

Some people ask me how it feels, getting to this point in my career, completing three albums being nominated for a Grammy—getting recognition on that level for my music. That doesn't matter much to me. The difference between me, as an artist, and another who might put a lot of stock in those types of accolades is really all in my lyrics. You have to truly understand how real they are for me.

I have received a lot of awards from different places and whatnot for what I do musically, but honestly, every plaque and award is packed away somewhere in my garage. My focus is on making music that touches real people in these real streets in a real way. If at the same time my music happens to touch someone in an award committee sitting somewhere in a boardroom, that's good too, but my focus is on people like me—people who face trials in the realities of life. These are the people who need to know that whatever they are feeling in whatever situation, they are not alone. *There is someone who has walked this path before you, who may even be able to offer you insight about it.*

This music has become my outlet to speak about my life, to speak about what I've gone through, and to speak on the issues of society, the issues of humankind, and try to shine somewhat of a brighter light on those issues. I saw the power of music early in my career, and I'm humbled by it. So I treat it with respect. To be able to move people is what this craft is all about. You aim first to move their bodies and moods with rhythm and sound and then to move their minds with lyrics and ideas. Hopefully from there you are able to move them to something more positive in life itself. What was at one time not even a passing interest for me has become a serious passion. It's crazy how things happen. And it's even crazier how this all got started.

This music started consciously for me when I was about seventeen. I was just hangin' out at one of my boys' house, doing what I do. He had a little sound system that he used to play with on the weekends. And we would turn it on during the downtime and play around with it, doing our thing. It was just a way to kick it and have a good time. Nothing real serious.

I remember the first time I was really holdin' the mic and starting to record something. This was around the same time, same age. I'm at the spot, at my friend's house, and he was going to play out at this little party thing. So I was going to roll with him and have a good time. No biggie, right? The party jump-off was cool. He has his system and is rocking the spot with all the latest. The people are feeling it, and the energy is fire. There are some heads in here, most of them familiar. We're all swaying and enjoying the beats. Next thing I know, my boy is feeling the vibe and he yells, "We got K Marley on dub."

I'm not expecting that, but I think, *Cool, whateva.* I flow with it. Again, no one is here but a lot of friends anyway, so I see it as another casual situation that we're just doing for the fun of it all. No pressure. I get up and start feeling the rhythm. I touch up on the mic a lil' bit and start putting my thing on it. It was all good. It was being received. Not a problem.

There was this producer there that night that used to come by the way sometimes. His name was Carl Peterson. Carl hears my voice, and he steps to me and says, "You have a good tone. Anybody ever tell you that? You should come by the studio sometime and we can see what we can do."

It isn't serious for me at this point, so I easily say, "Cool." Again, no biggie. It's something to do.

So I start going up to the studio on the weekends, hangin' out. I go on Saturday and sometimes on Sunday. It just depends. Once we get in the studio, he throws some music on and we vibe to it and just see what comes. I do my lil' rhymes, and he listens to every nuance. I get the feeling he's trying to explore my voice, to see what it can do, and to see what can be done with it. After a while, he gives me tracks to take home and tells me to write some lyrics. I'm starting to get into it. My eyebrow is officially raised, peeping the whole thing out.

Then it really got started for me. I started dancehall DJ'ing. The music kind of had me open now. I was seeing other ways of expressing myself and having fun with it. It was even the DJ'ing thing that got me started on the singing side. It was another thing that I just fell into. I'm doing my DJ thing and have this dancehall track thumping hard, but to me it needs a hook. It just needs a hook and it will be perfect. So I kick this track to my boy Carl, telling him, "Listen for me at this here; it needs a hook. I'd like to get somebody on a hook."

Now I'm telling him this 'cause I know he knows people and I'm picking his brain for his thoughts on it all. I'm learning. I'm soaking up the craft of this thing. He listens and is feeling me, and he says, "A'ight. You sing and put it down, and at least we'll have a pilot—like a guide—for them to follow, as far as what you want them to sing."

So I do that. Not a problem.

Upon laying down the vocals, he says something to me. I'm not expecting it. But I will never forget it. He says, "Well.

You sound closer to your father than any one of your other brothers." That's exactly what he said to me. He then tells me I need to consider singing. I'm still doin' the DJ'ing thing, but a seed has been planted. And after that he really starts pressing me about it. He tells me that I should see what's up, so eventually I start trying to sing and start to write lyrics to songs and melody verses to the hard-core DJ'ing music. Again, I'm just flowing with what comes. That's how it all happened for me.

This takes me back to one of the first songs I wrote. It was while writing this song, in particular, that I decided to start taking it seriously. This song made all the difference. What I wrote was a song, a tribute, and a communication to the man I wished I could talk to throughout all of these years. I wrote a song called "Dear Dad." It was just me expressing myself about how I felt about my father and losing him at a young age. I just put together all of the things I wanted to say and couldn't say. It was my first song.

I remember reaching for that song, "Dear Dad." It was a crazy experience and a healing one. I hadn't really dabbled around in my emotions like that. It was the perfect way to get out what had been bottled up for so long. I didn't know how powerful this art form could be. So, I took it to the studio, and we recorded it. That was that. Done.

The first time I heard my song on the radio was in Miami. McKenzie was the one who put it on. At the time we were doing a live broadcast—an interview. He was playing the new song, and I was taping the interview at the same time. It was a cool lil' setup.

This dude calls up the line during the broadcast. It sounds like he's in his car, and he says he had to pull over. The next part . . . I don't know if I was ready for it. Jah be my witness, it was a grown man saying he had to pull over because he started crying. He says he started crying listening to the song "Dear Dad" because the things that I expressed in my lyrics are exactly how he feels. He had lost his father too—a couple of years earlier, not as young as I did. But he pulls over and he feels every emotion that I wrapped into that song. It sneaks up on him in a way that he has to steer his car off the highway and shed tears right there. I'm hearing the emotion in this man's voice, and at that moment I know that for me there's a strong possibility of something happening here. Here I am just expressing myself in my personal way about what I'm going through, and now I'm realizing that it's affecting a lot of other people. Wow. That was life changing. That opened my eyes up to some things.

So after that, on the show, the calls just keep coming in and it's pretty much a lot of the same thing. People tell me that they had lost their mother. The song is reaching them too. Others say that they lost their brother. If they are missing someone that they had lost, they call in to tell me about it. This really has an impact on me. And from that moment, after writing "Dear Dad," I realize, *Okay, well, maybe I have somethin' here that can be built upon—something that definitely could become a very bright future as far as music is concerned.*

That was the start of that. That's when I really decided that I was going to focus and do this. It was really something to know and just get how much I could emotionally move a person with the power of music. It was unbelievable. It was a discovery for me. This was starting to get serious.

In the same kind of scenario, that same song spurred another life-changing moment a couple of years later. I was in Scandinavia, and I was doing a live show or music fest concert. As I'm coming off stage, this man walks up to me, bawling. Literally bawling. The man isn't holding back any of his emotions, and I don't think he could if he tried. Hundreds of people are walking around us, and he is just fully in that space. And I'm standing with him while he's struggling to tell me his story. He is determined to share it with me.

He tells me that he too had lost his father, about a month earlier. He says his father was the only person he had in his life and that at the time of his passing he was contemplating suicide. *Wow.* He says, "I was sitting in a room with a revolver in my hand, crying and telling myself I was just going do it. I was going to take my own life because it was no longer worth living."

I'm caught. I'm shook. I'm listening to this man and he says for some reason, he doesn't know why, he was sitting there with the pistol and something told him to press Play on the CD player next to him. He tells me that, ironically, "Dear Dad" came on. And at this point, I'm thinking, *Whoa.* He says he sat and listened to the song, and in that moment and at that time, the act of him pressing Play and hearing that song saved his life. It slowed him down and got him to think about things in a different way. He says he doesn't know why he pressed Play on the CD player. He didn't know what was in there. He tells me that he thinks it was his father trying to reach out to him somehow, to soothe him.

This man is standing in front of me bawling, and it almost brings me to tears because I can literally feel his pain and realize he can somehow feel my pain too. That was definitely another life-changing moment.

This music thing is very powerful. That's the lesson I was getting from this. I was learning how powerful this tool is—this tool that's now in my hands. It's moving people halfway across the world who are struggling with life-and-death situations. That's a whole different level.

So this all started when Carl Peterson, that producer, stepped to me at the little party. We had words. He was the person who actually started me in this music business, the one who started to groom me at that young age. As a producer, he understood how to record, how to control the voice, the notes, and all the basics that you need. So he kind of taught me about all that. I'm guessing at that point that he saw something in me that I couldn't see in myself and that a lot of people around me were unable to see. He is the one I really credit with starting my music career and with building me to the point of where I started to understand the progression of music.

This is all amazing because "music" is supposed to be the family business. I just never saw it like that for me until it was all just happening. I was solid in sports and the streets. Music was just not where my head was. And all of a sudden, one thing led to another and then another. I was just in the flow of it.

Even though I was only into sports, I was still listening to music and enjoying it as a consumer while growing up. I did have an appreciation for it; I just never thought of myself as a creator of it. But I guess when you step back and look at the eclectic range of music I was a fan of, you could kind of see the seeds of the whole thing.

The funny thing is that growing up in Jamaica there was only one radio station and one TV station. So sometime after we moved to the States, my mom bought one of those boom boxes for me. I was excited. This was some big thing for me. I take the boom box home, plug it in, and start scrolling the tuner until I come onto a station. It sounds cool, so I lock into it.

Now the funny thing is, the whole time I'm thinkin' there is only one radio station in all of Miami and all of America because there's only one station in Jamaica. Right? So I'm ready to get it crackin' with some musical vibes, no matter what they are. I'm just happy to hear some music, right?

Poor people are far from choosy because we never have the luxury to be so. The first thing I find, I stay on.

The station I tuned into in Miami was Y100. Today Y100 plays only soft rock and tracks like that. Cool. But back then, that radio station is playing Bon Jovi, Guns N' Roses, and George Michael—all of that. And George Michael was my favorite artist growing up as a little-bitty-ass kid. Well, him and Michael Jackson. I loved that shit! Can you imagine the son of Bob "Tuff Gong" Marley running around singing George Michael's greatest hits? Bananas, right? That was the funniest, but that's what they played on the station I got tuned in to. It was just the love of hearing some good music.

So as I'm listening to this music, it's striking a different note in me because it is all so different from what I was used to hearing back in Jamaica. It uses a different set of instrument sounds, it is creative, it is different from my dad's reggae, and it came with a lot of lyrical stories that I really got into. I loved the stories they came with, and I got attached to that kind of music. Straight up. That's the truth.

It isn't too long after that I finally hear some hip-hop. That shit just comes in and kills the game. That shit is hot. I love that. The first song I fell in love with in the hip-hop genre was Run DMC's "You Be Illin.'" *What?* Yeah, and I'm on that from then on. In the early years, my two favorite artists were Run DMC and LL Cool J, and I got way into their music. Who didn't? It was the music of the street and the new anthems of the ghettos. Just like my father's music was in his day.

I am glad it all happened like that because I make that kind of music now and the reaction I get is overwhelming. It's music that I feel too—music that I love creating and that comes naturally to me. Like I said, I love having freedom of expression in whatever music I'm feeling, and if I have the ability to do it, then why not?

Every legendary artist out there is an artist who took his or her craft its own way and didn't conform to what society was expecting or conform to what was on the radio playlists at the time. So I kind of try to follow the freedom of that mind-set. I just try to create my own sound, have my own image, and speak of things in ways that maybe wouldn't be common or plain, the same or expected. Just honest music.

Even in the early part of my career, when I started working on my first album and I did the rap thing and did a little soul. And, of course, I had some Rastas who used to come out on me, negatively talking the music down. But it was like that music wasn't what I was supposed to be doin' or I was only supposed to carry on my father's legacy and play the exact music he played in the way he played it. So I thought, *Okay, well, if I was to do that, then what would you say?* The only thing anyone would say would be, "Here goes Ky-Mani trying to be like his father. He's unoriginal. He really doesn't have anything to add or contribute to music." You can't win for losin' when it comes to people with that type of criticism. Critics just do what they do—they criticize. It doesn't matter what you're doing; they're bent on having something to say that subtracts. It doesn't mean you gotta listen to that garbage when it's being woofed at you. I just keep growing and doing me. They can "spectate" and comment till their last breath. I take my flow my own way, my own route. I continue the legacy with positive messages that uplift and illuminate the realities of what's goin' on out here, but I'm expressing it a bit differently. It can be a little aggressive at times and mellow at other times, but at the end of the day, it's me. Who else should it be?

I have really taken on paying attention to the world of music in a new way, to being a student of the music itself. I don't mean I pay attention to the music as artful sound only; I also know my fans and pay attention to what kinds of music they listen to other than me. I am the type of person who actually interviews my fans. I want to know what moves them, other than the songs that I sing. "Who else are you listening to? Are you listening to Pink Floyd? Are you listening to Pink? Pac?" I just want to know what else motivates people, and I would like to tap into that in some way. I have major respect for my audience. They're the ones who pay my bills. They're the real bosses.

Anybody will tell you that if I get off stage and there are 1,000 people lined up to take a picture, have an interview, or get an autograph, no matter how I'm feelin', I'm gonna sit there and sign 1,000 autographs. I will not turn anyone back or turn anyone down. I'm not that dude. Now at other times I might try to run off stage before that whole thing gets started because I know once it starts I ain't gonna stop. But it doesn't happen that way often. We do what we gotta do. If people take the time to come see me and stand in long lines to get an autograph, I for damn sure can take the time to sit and sign that piece of paper for them.

Bottom line, when it comes down to this music and my art, I'm always trying to do it in a different way. I believe that there are many styles, many approaches, to moving people at their soul level and there are many ways of continuing the core of my father's legacy and delivering his message to the world. There are many mansions in my father's house to inhabit. Even he was a fuse of the genres and musical styles of his time. This is not just one-dimensional. I'm always looking to learn and find different ways and new approaches, keeping it unorthodox.

When I finished my album titled *Radio* we were looking for a promotional tour to go out on. My booking agent comes at me with the most backward-ass-sounding idea: "Ky-Mani. Van Halen is going out on the road. Would you like to go?"

Okay, wait. Think about this. Think about the person who's walking into the record store right now to pick up a Ky-Mani Marley CD, and then look across the store and see the other person who has just walked in to buy a Van Halen CD. Look at them. Do the two of them look like they are about to go out and have a frickin' beer together?

So, of course, I say, "Ahhhhhhh, noooooo."

And I'm thinking *no* because I know this record, *Radio*, that I had just recorded and wanted to promote is as far away from Van Halen as you can get, I guess—unless I was doing polka music. That's one more step to the left.

But then, I think about this other new album that I'm working on that has a flipped sound from what my fans are used to from me. I have been recording these songs over the years on a different vibe—almost like an alternative, laid-back rock sound that has more of a guitar-driven feel. And I haven't played these songs for anybody. They are all fresh recordings, unexposed.

So, I reconsider and say, "Okay. I'm gonna take the show."

And the reason I take the show is I've always tried to bill and build myself as an artist who could go on any stage, no matter where it is, no matter who is in the audience, no matter what the musical style is—and connect. So if it's a reggae concert, I'm supposed to be able to go there, have that material, and be relevant. If it's a hip-hop show, same thing. If it's a rock-and-roll ticket, same thing. So accepting this opportunity is more like accepting a challenge. It is a challenge of something I have to prove to myself.

Right before I'm going out, I start reading the blogs. And everybody in the blogs is asking, "How is this going to work? How are they gonna put reggae with Van Halen? This is such garbage." I remember one where somebody writes in and asks, "Why are they giving us the lineup on this pamphlet thing?" And another person answers, "It's for us to ball up and throw at the opening act." I crack up. I laugh my ass off! It is the funniest thing. I think, *Okay, these people got jokes.* I already knew that they are about to get what's not expected from me, so it is all cool for me. I'm looking forward.

I go out on our first night on tour, and I play this song called "Real Love," along with some other songs that are like this acoustic guitar–driven thing. My first set is about thirty minutes. We do our thing. And I come off stage to a standing ovation at my first show on the tour. The first show, where I'm supposed to be getting persecuted, burned at the stake, and stoned, I leave to a standing ovation. It's a good feeling. And personally, it's a victory—a personal one and a creative one. This is the first time that I am playing this new material to a public audience and it worked. Here are fresh sets of ears that have never heard the material before and have never heard me before. Hell, they don't know me from Oprah, but they were feeling it. And for the next few months, every night we go out and do the same things. We blow away expectations. It's crazy. I'm lovin' it.

In the middle of the tour, one of the crew members comes to me and says, "Hey, let me tell you something. You know you're the only act that has ever lasted this long with them, right? Usually a band is out here with them no longer than three or four weeks, tops."

I didn't know that. And I had been with them for five months at this point. I'm there until I pull myself off the tour.

It was a great experience for me. It confirmed for me that I had the ability to walk out on a whole different stage, in front of a different audience, and be just like I said—relevant.

During that time, I had a pretty candid conversation with David Lee Roth. This is after we had a little drama on the tour with some roadies stuck on some lil' racist-type shit—some shit that David and Van Halen quickly squashed. So David and I are sitting in his dressing room, kicking it and talking about the little incident, talking about my dad, and he lets me know where he stands with all of the drama going on. He basically tells me not worry about it and that he'll personally take care of it—and he does. But the funny thing is that the next day his manager comes to the bus and says, "David said to give this to you," and he hands me a gift. It's one of those vintage model toy airplanes. I think, *Look at this. This is nice.* Then I notice something under the wings, where the missiles might go. David had tied some fat joints under each wing with some rubber bands. Four joints. I laugh my ass off. It was a great surprise. The little toy plane doesn't need jet fuel to get up high. It is going "green" buddy.

The tour was a good thing and a good time. It was a way outside the box from what was expected from me. And that's the way I like to keep it—growing, expanding, moving into new areas. This new record will definitely play around in that playground. For that reason, I plan to do a double album—both for my fans who love *Radio* and enjoy the edgy shit that I do and for those who love that alternative stuff.

Looking back now over my life, it all makes me wonder whether going that long and not discovering the hidden musical talent that was there in me had something to do with being outside of the family support and family embrace when I was coming up. I was rebelling against everything at the time, and music could have been one of those things. It probably was. But I guess it was going to the studio and playing around with the tracks, the sounds, and the songs, trying things out, that started to turn something on in me, something that was already there. I simply started trying some things musically, and it was being received. I think step by step this took me onto a platform where I started to believe more in myself. I think it also started to motivate me in a different way about life. Maybe it saved me.

Music is obviously the family business and I'm the son of Bob Marley. Therefore you would think that music would have been my first thought. But for the first half of my life, I wasn't living life like a son of Bob Marley. I was just another face on the block, trying to survive with the best of them. Period. So now, let's see how high I can fly with a destiny discovered.

Ninth Lesson Learned:

"You may run. You may even hide for a while. Destiny will find you either cowering in fear, or courageous and ready to take it by the hand, trusting you were meant to go where it goes and flow where it flows."

10

Life from Both Sides
(www.LoveOverAll.org)

I'VE SEEN LIFE NOW FROM BOTH SIDES. The best. The worst. The haves. The have nots. I've known both walks. I've traveled both paths. I've created both sets of footprints as a journeyman in this life. And this has caused me to see life from a very uniquely tailored perspective. I've been made to see the world from the shadows, and now I've walked with those who live lives enriched in the full light of day. And there is one thing that I have become clear about. The distance between these two worlds of human reality is not as far as you might imagine. The road is not as jagged and winding as many might choose to perceive it. The short distance between the two is straight and narrow. The only bridge between the two worlds is the heart, the thought and the act of love.

I believe that the problems of your world and mine—the little worlds that are our families and the larger world that is the family of humanity—are rooted in one simple solution . . . love. One love. Where there is one without food, there is always one with more than his or her share, full and fattened and discarding the excess. Where there is one who is uneducated, there is always another somewhere brimming with information and eagerness to teach it . . . but reluctant to teach it where the need for his or her knowledge exists the most. And this has become the pattern of our societies. People are closed off and self-indulgent, truly thinking that another man or woman with faces unlike theirs are in fact not just other versions of themselves in another circumstance.

I've walked the ghettos and have seen potential brilliance cast away like seeds planted away from the sunlight—away from that which would give them rise into a new creation of themselves, that would bring them up as fruit to benefit the world. This occurs because those who live in the world of light have been taught that there is truly a difference between themselves and the others, and they build tall walls to separate themselves physically, mentally, and politically. These walls keep the light of life from shining into the shadows cast upon these less fortunate seeds that could benefit us all. And because of this, we all suffer.

The future scientist who holds the simple cure to AIDS has been born but is languishing in the shadows, the ghettos, the shanty towns, ridden with simple survival concerns. His or her potential goes unrealized for a lifetime, leaving us all to suffer a blight and plight for yet another generation. The future political figure who has the skill and diplomacy to unlock the minds of the masses and shepherd our activities and thinking into the best use for ourselves has been born but is wasting away in the shadows, knowing not who he or she is because no light of love and no water of knowledge has hit this seed to show what gifts he or she has waiting inside to bring a new day of relations to human life.

For every problem, I believe a solution has been given, but we have not built a bridge or repaired the broken pathways between the parts of our human family that hold everything that we are looking for: a better life. We don't create this alone. We create this together. And when we don't, we all suffer. Not just the poor man, but the rich man who dies of cancer or multiple sclerosis in his castle, because he failed the shine the light on the one who was born with the scientific genius to cure his disease. Both men die as a result of the same crime to humanity—the crime of unrealized potential. A man like Dr. Ben Carson, who is the top neurosurgeon in the world, grew up in the ghettos of Detroit. But what would have happened to all the lives he saved had he not been brought out of the darkness by someone's love? Dr. Carson is not the only brilliant person who walks these broken communities where people lie in waste—these communities like that where I was born that are thrown away like the garbage of humanity. I was supposed to be flushed like Dr. Carson was supposed to be. But we made it out. Yeah. Now what about all the millions who are still in this dumpster of life? They are no different than me. I am no different than them. And you, no matter what your heights of society, are no different. You are just a product of your environment like every other human being is. And when environments are enriched, people are naturally enriched and new possibilities come to birth. I've seen life from both sides now.

I am *most* passionate about this. If people could learn to give a damn about people other than themselves, the grief of millions could end overnight. It's not that we need to give things to people. We just need to provide clear opportunity—clear, unobstructed, encouraging opportunity. Our problems are not complex. Our unwillingness to look beyond ourselves is complex. Opportunity is all that a human being needs to achieve all that he or she was born to do and become. Sometimes that means education, sometimes it means resources, and sometimes it means just knowing that somebody gives a shit about you after it seems that the world has thrown you away. The barrier to this is selfishness. The bridge to this is love.

Human beings can grow on their own if you give some of that up. And the funny thing is that once you give, you get even more back in return. Giving up some love does more for you than it does for the person you're giving it to. And it's this mentality today that I am building my life upon—this is the foundation upon which I want to build a lasting legacy that brings real *impact* to *real* people. Real impact . . . to real people. The mentality and philosophy of "One Love."

I think my passion for this pumps through my heart so strong because it is in my blood, coursing throughout my body. It specifically brings to mind my grandmother, Thelma Henlon, the woman she is, and of course my dad, the man he was and is in spirit right now.

A man who lives only for himself is already dead, right? I think about how I grew up in a cramped household that was nine deep. And today I know that there are many families who would refuse to live like that, and *somebody* has ended up on the street. It's crazy, but it's true. As poor and as utterly broke as we were, my grandmother never cooked a meal for us without feeding the baser who lived in the bushes across the street as well. I'm talking about the baser (head) named Bo who lived across the street in Liberty City in the bushes. This is the type of example I saw growing up, all around me. No matter what your conditions were, we knew that food is the staff of life, so if we had it to give you, we weren't going to deprive you of that. I was raised to understand that. I was raised under the philosophy of always giving a helping hand when you can. And even when you can't, you *still* put that helping hand out and you sacrifice yourself. You may have it today. Tomorrow, you may not. And the same one you are pulling up today, may one day have to pull *you* up. All of this was instilled in me.

I think I was instilled with the blessing of loving humanity in this way. It was instilled in me through the examples of my grandmother, the legacy of my father, and the early teachings and readings that my mother nurtured me with. I love people. I love when people are doing good. I hate seeing bums on the street—not because I'm in any way disgusted by them, but because I wish it didn't have to be like that. I'm that person who, in many ways, wants to save the world—the *entire* world. I see the displaced daily, and I've never passed a beggar or somebody who is homeless and not feel that. I look at it as somebody in dire need of help and that's what my spirit is about. It's about helping people. Every time I witness that, it bothers me. I wasn't given lessons on this; I got examples.

Whenever I would hear stories about my father when he was alive, that's exactly what I would hear about. I would hear about his work ethic, his love for humanity, his giving heart. People would tell me stories about him sitting at the foot of his doorstep and passing out money to the entire community for kids to go to school in Jamaica. I'm not talking about twenty or thirty people. I'm talking about hundreds of people who used to line up and come into the yard before school time. And there he would be on his step with a bag of money, passing the money out. This is what I mean by examples.

My mom always told me what kind of person my dad was. She told me all that he wanted out of life and shared some of his views on life. She told me about his whole vision of returning to Africa, where our people were originally from; she told me how he wanted his children to be productive members of society on a global scale. It was like that. But every corner I turn, wherever he has walked before me, I hear of these same stories about him. And I hear them especially in Jamaica. I get those kinds of stories every time.

When in Jamaica, we go into the Garrisons, into the heart of the hood, and hear how my father would open his trunk and give money away. Real charity on the ground with real people. This was back in the area where he was raised up, Trenchtown. He'd go to the hood, and if you needed help, he was there to help you. If he made some money, you could have it. My dad was never really a fussy type of guy. He wasn't one of the dudes who says, "Okay, I'm rich, so I'm gonna come flaunt my riches in front of you." He wasn't that dude. He came and he shared his wealth, and he shared it with the entire country. Everywhere you go, you hear the same stories . . . the same thing. "Your dad came and paid my hospital bill when I was on my sick bed and didn't know if I was gonna get out." "I was losing my house, and your dad came up with the money . . . and he bought the house." I hear these stories all the time. And some of these stories have come to me in the craziest of ways.

One story came to me from a police officer back in my juvenile delinquency days in Miami, back when I was living in the shadows of this thing. The cop had caught me tossing an ounce of marijuana as he was pursuing me. I was busted cold. Everything was against me, legally, and I was about to catch a real case. As I was stopped—caught and certain to go to jail—the cop just all of a sudden decided to do the unthinkable. *He let me go.*

We were in Miami, but that cop just happened to originally be a Jamaican. This is some other world type of shit . . . listen to this. The man turned to me and looked at me. You gotta hear me on this. He said, "The reason I'm letting you go now is that when I was a little boy, I was walking home from school one day . . . I was walking from school in the rain and your pops was passing me in the opposite direction. He turned around and asked me where I was going and I told him. And without any question he picked me up and brought me home." *Wow.* This is how I know I am destined to do what I am doing in life. I don't walk alone. I guess I never have.

When you're in Jamaica, on every corner you turn, there are many people who tell you stories like this. It's crazy to me, like the fact that this man, my father, has long been gone from our physical presence and yet I'm still receiving these blessings from him today.

So I'm trying to live my life in that in that sense. Because when my time comes . . . when my number is called . . . I want to have left a mark on the Earth. When somebody sees my child out, I want my child to hear, "Your dad was a good man. And my life was bettered because of him."

I want to be able to leave that same legacy, because that same love, that same example, is still paving the way for me today. It has been a bridge to safety in so many instances in my life.

And I'm not just talking about doing this work solely through my music. You can still be a great musician and be an asshole. In fact, there are a lot of those out there. But I'm talking about how you perform the music of your life . . . in your life. How you live it with people. This is my core passion in life. This is what motivates me. This is who I am. This is what moves me and gets me up to do what I'm doing every day in life, the possibility to contribute to people on this level.

Like I tell the children of LOAF (Love Over All Foundation, www.LoveOverAll.org), which is the new foundation that I have started, first and foremost, search yourself. Know who you are. Know your passions. Know what motivates you in life. Know what it is that you're good at and just work toward that. Just work toward perfecting that. Have an open mind and be a go-getter. And then, *get it.* I tell the children all the time, if you want something, fight for what you want. Don't let people tell you that you can't have or can't become anything. It's not up to them. It's up to you.

I have always been the type of person to charitably give. And I don't mean the structured, organized charity. I mean helping those who are in need under any circumstances that you see—in circumstances that you know right now. This even goes for those on the street. I have had people approach me and say, "Okay, well, my daughter is in the hospital and I need [such and such] to help." If I had it, I would always extend a helping hand. Always.

With the strong sense and urge to help people, I decided to start my own foundation, an idea that a friend of mine, Chez, or *Ché* as we call him, indirectly helped me develop. We had been talking about it for quite some time.

Ché was running a sports club in Jamaica about ten years ago and I shared with him some of the things I thought he should try to implement. At one time, he was bringing some equipment down to Jamaica on Sport Day for the kids in the school, and I told him he shouldn't donate it all to the school. I told him he should give some of it to the police and then let them give it to the school as if they were the ones donating. He didn't like that idea, and honestly he told me point blank, "No way. Fuck them."

I understood where he was coming from, but I said, "Yeah fuck them, but you know you still need their asses on your side too, bruh."

I reminded him that when you give, more comes back to you than you can imagine.

With that being said, he took my advice and he did it. He gave it all up to the police. I was proud of him. And I think it was no more than a month later when he came to me and said point blank, "That was the best advice *anybody* has ever given me."

It ended up working out in his favor in the long run, and now he has been doing it for a couple of years. His actions earned him both the respect of the community and the respect at the police department. He gave the police in the community an opportunity to show themselves in a new light. And something happened on both sides. The police now will police in a new way. And the community now will see them in a new way . . . maybe less as enemies and more as possible helpers in times of need. Not to mention, Ché now runs around town with no difficulties to carry on his mission. He has a nearly free pass to do it all as he pleases and run his program with no problems.

Gathering inspiration from this success, in February 2009, I launched my foundation and we launched it in full gear and regalia. We held a huge fund-raiser that was co-sponsored by us and the Prince of Monaco. We couldn't have been happier with the results and excitement this brought to our cause. It was attended by the likes of Denise Rich and Julian Lennon, among others. Denise made a great contribution, and Julian bought a guitar at the charity auction for 20,000 Euros. Both tremendously helped the launch. It was a great time.

My family and I are involved in many causes. We've performed at events sponsored by the United Nations. We participated in the Africa Unite event in Addis Ababa,

Ethiopia, which was celebrating the sixtieth birthday of my dad. I've also performed for and supported United Nations' fund-raisers in New York that address so many global issues that affect us all, such as AIDS and the scourge of human trafficking.

During our foundation's launch, I returned to Falmouth and went out to the school there. I saw the conditions that the kids were in, and it wasn't the greatest. But man, the kids were very eager to learn. The first time I went, I passed out some achievement medals and gave a short speech. I saw and felt the energy and vibration that those kids were giving off. I felt overwhelmed and wanted to help even more. It made me want to give them a chance to have some of the simple opportunities I could clearly see they were lacking.

We went out to play soccer, and the entire team was playing without shoes. Since I was in a position where I could help, I decided to. I love to give a child an opportunity so that he or she can make the best of it. Later I can look back and say, "Wow. It really paid off." I'm not looking for anything in return per se, but my blessings will come from a greater power in return. I wouldn't do this for media coverage or a write-up—none of that simple bullshit matters. It's all for the greater good. And like I said . . . I've seen life from both sides now. I know what can be done.

I am proud to have established my own foundation now. Like I said, Love Over All Foundation (LOAF; www.Love OverAll.org) has been up and running for about a year now and is growing. The work is still in progress, and I am really excited about it. I'm seeing that all that these kids need is an outlet to be plugged into. That's all they need. Just a chance.

For example, many kids in my hometown can't go to school because their mothers don't have the money to pay the small school tuition and can't afford the uniform. These mothers are suffering, so you find many of their seven- and eight-year-olds on the corner beggin' when they're supposed to be in school, all because that mother is sufferin'. These mothers need all the help they can get, so they send their kids to the corner to go beg for food and pennies instead of sending their children to school or trying to help develop their education. It's crazy out here, for real. Crazy. I would like to set up a system where I can go and help these children get into schools. We can take it upon ourselves to pay their school fees and to make sure that every child has two or three pairs of school uniforms, school shoes, and other school supplies. Whatever it is, I am definitely going to be a part of it.

As far as my legacy . . . music, acting, or other . . . I want to be remembered as a humanitarian. I can see no other worthy legacy. I want to be remembered as an artist who came and left a mark—a positive mark. I want to be remembered as an artist who came and produced music that reflected reality, had substance, and provided inspiration to change one's reality into a new reality. This desire is what comes naturally to me.

The foundation leg of my journey is new, and what we've started doing so far is refurbishing schools in Jamaica. The first one I went to was my old school in Falmouth, Trelawny; it's called Falmouth All Age School. I repainted the school in February 2009, around the time we launched LOAF.

Since then, I traveled back to Falmouth and I bought lunch for 920 students. And I've decided to do that every February. I am now in the process of purchasing their sports jerseys, their soccer jerseys, and their netball jerseys. We're also invested in building a track. The next project is to establish music lessons on Saturdays so that these kids can develop their talents—an effort to bring some light to these seeds. We are planning to have three sessions on Saturdays, which would teach these kids a variety of music—piano, guitar, voice, or whatever.

What I'm realizing is that there are many children in these situations everywhere, situations that they are born into beyond any fault of their own. They are outstanding children, many of whom are already blessed with talent and ability but have not yet been given a chance or an opportunity to build on that talent. That's it. It's that simple. And many of them have talent in an area but don't even know it because they haven't had an opportunity that let's them experiment and discover it. They need to see these talents in themselves. They need to see it in order to generate hope that they can work toward something better in their lives, that they and their families can outgrow the conditions they find themselves in. Simple.

We are also working on a health initiative to help families and children struggling with healthcare issues. I have two boys with sickle cell anemia, and I've witnessed firsthand what they endure and the pain they feel. My being there and being helpless is the absolute worst feeling I've ever had, to see a child in pain and be unable to do anything about it. I also have a daughter who is challenged with diabetes. And I've watched her in a diabetic coma twice already. These issues touch home for me. These medical issues are another thing I'm looking forward to working on—whatever it is that I can do to help. On my last album, *Radio*, I thought of linking the album with the Sickle Cell Foundation to donate a portion of the proceeds from each sale. On my next album, coming up, I definitely want to secure that partnership with the Sickle Cell Foundation to share the royalties. My goal is to set up my whole life in ways that allow me to always be helping.

My two boys receive monthly blood transfusions. Every month we take them to the hospital to go through this involved process to get their transfusions. These have tremendously helped reduce the pain they would otherwise experience and the subsequent crisis. Ever since we started doing this, it has broken the cycle of crisis and left us with a new breakthrough. So far, so good. But many other families are struggling with this and don't have the resources I have to get this level of health care for their own children. Too many. Countless. I want to help families dealing with significant health issues.

I want be one of those people who present these opportunities to all kids. And although there are not so many yet, I want to dedicate my life to being *one more*. One reason, of course, is that this is what my father was all about. And yes, this is what he would want. But another reason is that this is just a part of me. It's in my blood and bones. It's in my DNA, my fiber. If I'm his seed, I figure I should be living my life to complete his unfinished business. Living and spreading the philosophy of "One Love."

I'm completely passionate and committed to this. It's not hard to be. There is need all around us—everywhere. And many of us have the *means* to fulfill the need. But do we have the *heart*? Do we have the will? If you wish to donate your own time, ideas, resources, and love, visit our website and make this journey with me.

I want to build a bridge from where I was to where I am, giving kids a chance to cross over to the other side. And seeing these realities from both sides, I know that the distance is not that far—I know that the bridge is just a little love.

Tenth Lesson Learned:

"All suffering occurs where love is not occurring."
"All the world's problems and all the world's solutions can be bridged in as short of a distance as the twelve inches between the hemispheres of your brains and the chambers of your heart."

Ky-Mani Marley
Songs-Lyrics

Hustler

Wowowowowooooo yeh
Wowowowowooooo yeh
Wowowowowooooo yeh

I can't work a nine to five
Baby I'm a hustler, I'm a keep hustling
Rather risk my freedom and my life
Baby I'm a rider, I'm a keep riding
I got my future infront my eyes, and the fight is to survive
Baby this is just my life

So, pass me the chalice mek mi burn it up
I know you feel my vibes so baby turn me up
We livin in a time that's so corrupt
So I do what I gotta to break bread
It's 101 shottaology
Burn di pigs and mi she dat without apology
Movement haffi gwan, money haffi mek

And if a suh it haffi go den wah

Food haffi tek yeh

Making a run through the states

But I'll be back shortly girl with food for the plates

So don't worry, just say a prayer for me

Girl I know that you're a rider for me

One time let's go

I can't work a nine to five

Baby I'm a hustler, I'm a keep hustling

Rather risk my freedom and my life

Baby I'm a rider, I'm a keep riding

I got my future infront my eyes, and the fight is to survive

Baby this is just my life

Woo, beautiful come let me give you my love

Your cup is running over I keep pouring my love

When the heathen rise against I, I kill them with love

Rastafari guide and bless us and protect us with love

You're nothing less than royalty, so I provide
you with pure love and loyalty

I know you worry girl when I'm in the street, but
understand me, that's the way that I eat

One time and let's go

I can't work a nine to five
Baby I'm a hustler, I'm a keep hustling
Rather risk my freedom and my life
Baby I'm a rider, I'm a keep riding

And if I gotta do a little time away
Tell me that you'll keep the faith

And don't you worry I got lots put away
So everything will be ok
Girl we'll be ok
So you got my love, girl do you follow me
I'm a student want to study your anatomy
I'm a rebel that's burning up all dem policies

Babylonians cannot lead us a stray
No way, no day
I come fi turn on the agony
Ghetto youths are getting wiser to their strategies
Dollars a run and everybody living happily
And that's the way it should be

I can't work a nine to five
Baby I'm a hustler, I'm a keep hustling
Rather risk my freedom and my life

Baby I'm a rider, I'm a keep riding
I got my future infront my eyes, and the fight is to survive
Baby this is just my life

So, pass me the chalice mek mi burn it up
I know you feel my vibes so baby turn me up
We livin in a time that's so corrupt
So I do what I gotta to break bread
It's 101 shottaology
Bun di pigs and mi she dat without apology
Movement haffi gwan, money haffi mek
And if a suh it haffi go den wah
Food haffi tek yeh
Making a run through the states
But I'll be back shortly girl with food for the plates
So don't worry, just say a prayer for me
Girl I know that you're a rider for me
One time let's go

I can't work a nine to five

Country Journey

Gotta go . . .

I really wanted to take you with me
on my little country journey
but you have to understand, oh why
and not sit alone at home and cry,
and cry, alone at home and cry

Even though you're not here by my side
truely you're always on my mind
so i just called to sing a lullabye
to comfort your heart so you never cry

I really wanted to take you with me
on my little country journey
but you have to understand, oh why
and not sit alone at home and cry,
and cry, alone at home and cry

I really wanted to take you with me
on my little country journey
but you have to understand, oh why
and not sit alone at home and cry,
and cry, alone at home and cry . . .

Tell her not to worry you'll be okay
she should pray for your safety night and day
soon back together you'll be again
i know you both can't wait to see that day

I really wanted to take you with me
on my little country journey
but you have to understand, oh why
and not sit alone at home and cry,
and cry, alone at home and cry

I really wanted to take you with me
on my little country journey
but you have to understand, oh why
and not sit alone at home and cry,
and cry, alone at home and cry . . .

Wherever you are just call his name
he'll hear your voice and it'll make his day

a day doesn't pass, when you're not on his mind
please don't cry, you'll be together in time

Even though you're not here by my side
truely you're always on my mind
so i just called to sing a lullabye
to comfort your heart so you never cry

I really wanted to take you with me
on my little country journey
but you have to understand, oh why
and not sit alone at home and cry,
and cry, alone at home and cry

I really wanted to take you with me
on my little country journey
but you have to understand, oh why
and not sit alone at home and cry,
and cry, alone at home and cry . . .

I really wanted to take you with me
on my little country journey
but you have to understand, oh why
and not sit alone at home and cry,
and cry, alone at home and cry . . .

I really wanted to take you with me
on my little country journey
but you have to understand, oh why
and not sit alone at home and cry,
and cry, alone at home and cry.

Don't cry.

One Time Lyrics

Motivated right about now

The vibe on fire

The track on fire

Well let me tell it to you one time

You violate me even one time

I only pull the trigger one time

Slug twist wig one time

You see the pigs just holla one time

Soldiers raise em and bus em one time

Girl if you give it to me one time

It's for sure you'll be back more than one time

Just know you fucking with a city boy

And you know dem city boys keep a lot a toys

Like AKs, SKs, Eagles and Nines

Keep me feelin like the world is mine

I'm at the crib, just dying for shit to pop off

So I can run in the safe and snatch the lock off

I got something that will run through your vest

Will leave a baseball hole in the chest

So fuck with me

My mama raised me as a soldier

Born, bread a soldier, Live, die a soldier

And you can't say I never told ya boy

Gorillas killing snitches for free

Who Me

I pledge allegiance to the hood b/c police and politicians
mean us no good

So light it up if you ready to fly, real soldiers ain't afraid to die

Smoke with me

Well let me tell it to you one time

You violate me even one time

I only pull the trigger one time

Slug twist wig one time

You see the pigs just holla one time

Soldiers raise em and bus em one time

Girl if you give it to me one time

It's for sure you'll be back more than one time

I'm fighting dem demons, confidently, courageous

I'm for the team not for individual status

It wouldn't be real if haters didn't hate us

So Step back fool, my flow is contagious

Here come the birth of a new era

I'm bout to bring them to a new level

Bring them through the heat of the night

Then guide em right back to the light

Stay with me

I'm riding high, I'm burning on the Cali cush

She got the goods, baby just need a little push

Raised in the south, my life is like a story book

A little faith, and soldier that was all it took

Look at them now, look at them how I got them shook

What it is is what it is

No matter how it look

I got the herbs if you ready to fly

Light up and let us head for the sky

Stay with me

Well let me tell it to you one time

You violate me even one time

I only pull the trigger one time

Slug twist wig one time

You see the pigs just holla one time

Soldiers raise em and bus em one time

Girl if you give it to me one time

It's for sure you'll be back more than one time

Damn I love the way you shining

Oooo girl, the true definition of a diamond

You make me wanna give you twins

I'm at your door, baby please let me in

Good God you got me feening

That coco butter got the sexy body gleaming

And I only need it one time

And fo sho you'll be back more than one time

And when I roll, I roll by myself

But fool don't get it twisted, get beside yourself

Cause I'll feed your grains that aint good for your health

No silly rabbit just kill his self yeh

Storm told me that he got me

PR said when it's done they gonna sweat me

My mama told me not to let them cowards get me

I switched up now, I'm busin at em lefty

Well let me tell it to you one time

You violate me even one time

I only pull the trigger one time

Slug twist wig one time

You see the pigs just holla one time

Soldiers raise em and bus em one time

Girl if you give it to me one time

It's for sure you'll be back more than one time

Royal Vibes lyrics

And she said
And she said
And she said
Yeh Yeh she said
And she said
And She said
Woooooo

And she said
She's never been loved like this before
She's never been touched like this before
She's never felt feels like this before
She's in love with me.
And she said
She's never been loved like this before
She's never been touched like this before
She's never felt feels like this before
She's in love with me.
And she said

She love me fi di royal vibes wah mi bring

She loves me for the upful song dem wah mi sing

She said she loves me for

Inna di bed when we a make love she hear the angels dem a sing

And she said

She love me for this rasta life I'm living

She love me for she love the way me hail up the king

She say she love me for inna di moments of clutch I'm no punk

She love my gangsterism.

And I said

Girl I'll never dish you no wrong

Girl I'll never bring you no harm

Girl you're my good luck charm

You're the queen and I'm the king.

And she said

She's never been loved like this before

She's never been touched like this before

She's never felt feels like this before

She's in love with me.

And she said

She's never been loved like this before

She's never been touched like this before

She's never felt feels like this before

She's in love with me.

She would love to seize the moment
For she's longing for my touch
She is scared because in my past she's seen so much
She Still cares but to be with me will hurt so much

What good is to be together if between us there aint trust
And I said
Love will you forgive me, for I know I brought you harm
In my younger days my ego got in the way and I know I did you some wrong
Still I love that you're my empress, you're my good luck charm
So my word to you from this moment on
Is, Girl I'll never dish you no wrong
Girl I'll never bring you no harm
Girl you're my good luck charm
You're the queen and I'm the king

And she said
She's never been loved like this before
She's never been touched like this before
She's never felt feels so real before
She's in love with me.
And she said
She's never been loved like this before
She's never been touched like this before
She's never felt feels like this before
She's in love with me.

Chu

She love me fi di royal vibes wah mi bring

She loves me for the upful song dem wah mi sing

She said she loves me for

Inna di bed when we a make love she hear the angels dem a sing

And she said

She love me for this rasta life I'm living

She love me for she love the way me hail up the king

She say she love me for inna di moments of clutch I'm no punk

She love my gangsterism.

And I said

Girl I'll never dish you no wrong

Girl I'll never bring you no harm

Girl you're my good luck charm

You're the queen and I'm the king.

And she said

She's never been loved like this before

She's never been touched like this before

She's never felt feels so real before

She's in love with me.

And she said

She's never been loved like this before

She's never been touched like this before

She's never felt feels so real before

She's in love with me.

Warriors Lyrics

"One time for my warriors, my laaa smugglers and all my buffalo soldiers

One time for my warriors, my heat carriers and all my buffalo, yo
One time for my warriors, my laa smugglers and all my buffalo soldiers
One time for my warriors, my heat carriers and all my buffalo, hey

verse 1:
Say fool you must be crazy
What is it you tryin to do u cannot faze me
I've been smokin on a pound and feelin hazy
For five-o I wont stop they gotta chase me
Now make it mo' better for the cream
My music brings the cheddar, see what I mean
The seats in the ride is leather, the rims are clean
I change my @$!$% like the weather, now I'm the king, yeah yeah

"One time for my warriors, my laaa smugglers and all my buffalo soldiers
One time for my warriors, my heat carriers and all my buffalo, yo

One time for my warriors, my laa smugglers and all my buffalo soldiers
One time for my warriors, my heat carriers and all my buffalo, hey

verse 2:
Now if you wanna find me, I'll be in Jamaica smoked out
In a black navigator, evading all the playa haters—high
Here comes the rover with the troops
Decked out in army fatigues,
and stompin 'um with my black tin boots, say what
So while they're remixing punch lines, I create
How you wanna battle me, hah
When you just a feather weight, hey yo
You know how long I've been knocking out heavyweights, its best you chill
Meditate find your space and know your place because
I'm like a disciple, when i appear from the clouds
I get on stage I grab the mic and then I bless the crowd, blow
Me and my soldiers we gon' ride tonight
Get some of that sticky green we gon' get high
Babylon ridin slowly, ah try fe hold me
Want to prosecute i for my Ganja
Babylon ridin slowly, ah try fe hold me
Like they don't know, eh, well i'm tellin ya

"One time for my warriors, my laaa smugglers and all my buffalo soldiers
One time for my warriors, my heat carriers and all my buffalo, yo

One time for my warriors, my laa smugglers and all my buffalo soldiers
One time for my warriors, my heat carriers and all my buffalo, hey

verse 3:
It's me a runnin down in J-A
Twenty thousand pounds of Sess on the sea headin straight for the MIA
Now I'm a check the Ras around the way
hold a vibes and bun my Chalice and then meditate, hey
Now privately I hit the airways
I'm burnin laa 'til I touch down in the M-I-A, yeah
I call my soldiers from around the way
I call up Shorty for the party we be doin this everyday

"One time for my warriors, my laaa smugglers and all my buffalo soldiers
One time for my warriors, my heat carriers and all my buffalo, yo
One time for my warriors, my laa smugglers and all my buffalo soldiers
One time for my warriors, my heat carriers and all my buffalo, hey

"One time for my warriors, my laaa smugglers and all my buffalo soldiers
One time for my warriors, my heat carriers and all my buffalo, yo
One time for my warriors, my laa smugglers and all my buffalo soldiers
One time for my warriors, my heat carriers and all my buffalo, hey

Dear Dad Lyrics

Dear God,

I have a letter here from me to Dad and I want
to let you know it might be a little sad.

Dear God, I have a letter here from me to Dad and I want
to let you know ... Here it goes ...

Dear Dad I really didn't get to know you

Sometimes I sit and wonder and it makes me blue

There's one memory that stays on the back of my mind

And this memory has me thinking about you all the time

Oh Pa, I swear we miss you so

I wish you were here to see your boys grow

Incase you're wondering, mommy she's doing fine

And she tells me stories about you Papa all the time

So when I'm down and out

Lonely or just feeling blue

All I do Daddy Daddy is think of you

The thoughts alone erase my fears and dries my tears

I'm just writing to let you know that someone cares

Daddy I love you, really really love you

Daddy I miss you, I miss you and I know my brothers and sisters do too

I love you, really really love you

And I know you gave your love to the people

And some of who you thought you could trust, they deceived you

But betrayal brings another day

At least that's what my Mama says

And when I'm through I'll place this letter in the Bible

And I'll pray to Jah to send his disciples

To deliver you this letter

It will make I feel much better

And now I sing

Dear God, I have a letter here from me to Dad and I want
to let you know it might be a little sad.

Dear God, I have a letter here from me to Dad and I want
to let you know it might be a little sad.

PS. So much things I'd like to know

So much things to say

I'm going to save it because I know we'll be together someday

I'm just writing to let you know that we all care

And to let you know you left the whole world in tears

Daddy I love you, really really love you

Daddy I miss you, I miss you and I know my brothers and sisters do too

I love you, really really love you

Dear Dad I really didn't get to know you

Sometimes I sit and wonder and it makes me blue

There's one memory that stays on the back of my mind

And this memory has me thinking about you all the time

Oh Pa, I swear we miss you so

I wish you were here to see your boys grow

Incase you're wondering, mommy she's doing fine

And she tells me stories about you Papa all the time

So when I'm down and out

Lonely or just feeling blue

All I do Daddy Daddy is think of you

The thoughts alone erase my fears and dries my tears

I'm just writing to let you know that someone cares

Daddy I love you, really really love you

Daddy I miss you, I miss you and I know my brothers and sisters do too

So Hot Lyrics

Hahaha you know what time it is girl
What they sayin? they ain't sayin nothing
Tell it to her straight

[Chorus:]

Girl girl you so hot, you so hot
Like burning you, like burnin you
Girl you so hot, you so hot
Like burnin you, like burning you

Girl I like your style and your attitude
Yore polite yet you're so rude
I want to get in your head
Right before I get in your head

I got some things I wann do to ya
And something that's new to ya
I know you got a wild side

And baby I got a wild side
So back it up and let me put it on you
Ma with these eyes baby
What you gon do
Girl don't fight the feeling
Come over reach for the ceiling
The only thing I want to do is love you
And I promise to put nothing above you
Girl I see you're the real thing
And I know I'm the real thing

[Chorus]

Baby got a body like a fast car
She got me speeding like a nascar
She like it when I keep the wheels spinning
I'm getting real deep in the engine
She loves it hot, she loves it spicy
She love it when I'm running the girls nicely
Oh baby I'm a rider
And good god, gilr you on fire

Come and let me break you off
Break you off some of this ah ah
Girl just go ahead and take it off

So I can get to the na na
Oohh come and let me break you off
Break you off some of this ah ah
Girl go ahead and take it off
So I can get to the na na

Ohh wind with me grind with me
Oh girl don't fight it
Flow with me go with me
We're making love [x2]

[Chorus]

Tom Drunk Lyrics

Let me tell you of a story
About a preacher I once knew
Had a wife that was a teacher
And the daughter or was it two

He was loved among his neighbors
For the wonders works he's done
For the building of the new church
And the walk for homeless funds

But things change and times got rough
And his wife is acting strange
And the friends that Tom once knew so well
Just don't seem the same

Now Tom drunk
But Tom's no fool
Just keep it cool, Tom
And stick to the rules

Tom drunk
But Tom's no fool
Just keep it cool, Tom
And stick to the rules

Now instead of getting better
Things started to get worse
When they dropped off from the ministry
And burnt down Tom's new church

After all the things that Tom had done
It seems like no one cared
Now Tom is sitting all alone
Shedding lonely tears

Tom drunk
But Tom's no fool
Just keep it cool, Tom
And stick to the rules

Tom drunk
But Tom's no fool
Just keep it cool, Tom
And stick to the rules

To much stress, can't bare the pressure
So he sips the Devil's water
Reach at home, he rapes his wife
Then he turns and beats his daughter

Can't believe he grabbed his gun
Then he slowly cocked the hammer
Put the pistol to his head
Then he bowed and said the prayer

Oh, Tom, Tom, Tom, Tom, Tom
Tom is gone, Tom is gone
Oh, Tom, Tom, Tom, Tom, Tom
Tom is gone Tom is gone

Tom drunk
And played a fool
And lost his cool
His soul is in the deepest blue

Tom drunk
And played a fool
And lost his cool
His soul is in the deepest blue

Tom drunk
Played a fool
Tom is drunk now

Tom drunk
And played the fool
And lost his cool now
He lost his cool now

Tom drunk
And played the fool
And lost his cool now
His soul is in the deepest blue

Tom drunk
And played the fool
And lost his cool now
His soul is in the deepest blue, yeah, yeah

Notes

Notes